93

To Frank
from
[signature]
1975

MILLENNIUM MAN

Published by Bible Voice, Inc.
Van Nuys, California

MILLENNIUM MAN

MAN

by GEORGE OTIS

First Edition

TABLE OF CONTENTS

Dedicated to

Tom, Joan, Joe and Les'a Ingram

— *of Millennium quality*

ABOUT THE AUTHOR

Pat Boone says, "I met George after his adventure had already hit high gear. The excitement in his life, the radiance in his eyes, became a spiritual lighthouse. There is a dynamic in George — like a man with his finger in a high-voltage socket!"

George Otis' life could hardly have been better planned to prepare him to write *Millennium Man*. Twenty years as a senior executive in the electronic and aerospace fields laid a helpful scientific undergirding.

Millennium Man was a bold undertaking. Perhaps only a layman would feel the liberty to attempt such a colossal theme. George's credentials are adequate. He has traveled 500,000 miles over the past five years, as a lay-teacher, and has authored four major books.

George himself has said, *"Millennium Man* stands as the single most challenging and exhilarating research undertaking of my life."

PREFACE

MILLENNIUM, Literally a period of a thousand years, (a pseudo-Latin word formed on the analogy of *biennium, triennium,* from Lat. *mille,* a thousand, and *annus,* year). The term is specially used of the period of 1,000 years during which Christ, as has been believed, would return to govern the earth in person. Hence it is used to describe a vague time in the future when all flaws in human existence will have vanished, and perfect goodness and happiness will prevail. . .

Faith in the nearness of Christ's second advent and the establishing of his reign of glory on the earth was undoubtedly a strong point in the primitive church. . .

In Revelation . . . it occurs in the following shape (ch. XX). After Christ has appeared from heaven in the guise of a warrior, and vanquished the anti-Christian world-power, the wisdom of the world and the devil, those who have remained steadfast in the time of the last catastrophe, and have given up their lives for their faith, shall be raised up, and shall reign with Christ, on this earth as a royal priesthood for 1,000 years. At the end of this time Satan is to be let loose again for a short season; he will prepare a new onslaught, but God will miraculously destroy him and his hosts. Then will follow the general resurrection of the dead, the last judgment, and the creation of new heavens and a new earth.

—Encyclopaedia Britannica, Vol. 15, Pg. 495,6.

1

THE ELECTRIC PRIEST

"The man's a fool and I'm tuning him out! It grates me to have to sit here and listen to a LAYMAN trying to teach on, of all things, Millennium life. No clergyman should ever be subjected to this indignity from a layman." Thus went the thoughts of the fuming Catholic Priest during a recent meeting in Auckland, New Zealand.

Father John had been brought to the meeting from his parish, 70 miles south. He looked around the audience in College Meeting Hall and said, "Why, these people are spellbound! They're swallowing the man's teaching, even though he confessed never even going to seminary. These laymen's meetings, out from under clergy's control, can be dangerous. They seem to let anyone teach, and on just about anything at all. Besides, there just isn't much in the Bible about that era. The Millennium idea is so ethereal; why doesn't he stick to things that will help people now?"

Fr. John nudged the parishioner who had talked him into coming to Auckland on his Sunday afternoon off to hear this George Otis, and said, "Let's get out of here. This man is trying to teach on something no one knows about. The Millennium, huh! Come on, let's head back home."

His friend said, "Shhhhhh, I'd like to hear the rest. It's really interesting! Please hold on." The priest slumped back in the chair with his arms tightly folded and fumed until I had finished my message.

Monday dawned as one of those bright New Zealand sparklers. At the breakfast table Fr. John's thoughts turned back to the experience in last night's meeting. His repulsion had somehow grown even further during the night. John knew he should dismiss the whole episode from his mind, but there was something gripping about what he had heard about the Millennium. He said, "Just imagine the impudence of a layman spouting scripture and trying to interpret it to me, a man of the cloth. Laymen need the guidance of proven scholars."

Later that morning, while in the rectory, Fr. John opened his Bible. His eyes fell on II Pet. 1:20. The words struck like fire! "Knowing this first, that no prophecy of the scripture is of any private interpretation." He slammed the book shut and sat there transfixed. God seemed to be shouting to him, "The Holy Word is a direct communication to each of My children. I am prepared to interpret scripture to any sincere believer; clergyman or otherwise."

Fr. John said, "Why, Otis used that very same scripture yesterday! Strange I should stumble over a verse I never noticed before."

The following afternoon the priest was back in the rectory library sitting at a desk. He reached and drew from the shelf a volume on St. Francis of Assisi, one of the most towering and classic of Roman Catholic heroes. St. Francis had always been an inspiration to Fr. John. Some twenty minutes later the priest flinched:

The Saint was sharing about his own personal relationship with birds and animals. He wrote of a deep stirring in people to make friends with the wild things and how he believed this was a subconcious vestige from Eden days when Adam had joyous communion with the animals. St. Francis was telling how, in the Millennium, he believed there would be a restoration of man's fellowship with all creation. . . "St. Francis teaching on the Millennium?," mused the puzzled clergyman. He was awestruck! He had just pooh-poohed this same concept in George Otis' message! The layman's revelation had been identical to his own revered saint. It was haunting but still irritating. This Protestant must have "lucked out" in this part of his teaching.

"What does all this mean anyhow?" thought Fr. John. "Is God trying to say something to me?" He brushed it aside as coincidence and his anger toward the layman's teaching remained. . . .

The next day the priest looked at his calendar. It was Wednesday. He strode across the lawn and up the church steps. Fr. Roland greeted him just inside the sanctuary, "Good morning, Fr. John, how are you? I have a favor to ask. We have chosen you to represent the parish at a meeting downtown in Fellowship Hall tomorrow noon. There's a speaker in town for just one day and all faiths are collaborating in his meetings. It would be rude if our parish wasn't represented."

Fr. Roland handed Fr. John a folded yellow bulletin and said, "The time and particulars are printed on here, John. I appreciate your fulfilling this obligation for us."

The priest slowly straightened out the bulletin and turned it over — he nearly dropped it!

ONE DAY ONLY!
PRESBYTERIAN LAYMAN FROM U.S.A.
MEETING TIMES: 12 NOON & 7 P.M.
ALL DENOMINATIONS WELCOME
ADMISSION FREE
SPEAKER: GEORGE OTIS

Fr. John was speechless! This was getting ridiculous.

It was high noon on Thursday when Fr. John steamed into Fellowship Hall. About 100 special guests had gathered for the luncheon meeting. Prominent businessmen, pastors, Godfrey Bowen (the World's Champion Sheep Shearer), and others. The priest spotted his irritator standing in the midst of a cluster of people. The redheaded Catholic set a straight course for the group, like a destroyer at full speed.

He broke in, "Mr Otis, my name is Father John. I was one of the people in your audience last Sunday evening, in Auckland."

I turned to the priest and thrust out my hand. "Were you, really? It's good to meet you formally. Do you live in this city, Father?"

Fr. John never took my hand or even answered my question. "It would be less than honest if I didn't tell you how disturbed I was with your teaching on the Millennium. As a matter of fact, it has hung over me all this week. I'm here only because I was ordered to represent our parish. Mr. Otis, I'm a blunt man and you should know I couldn't in good conscience come here. I don't agree with your teaching; furthermore I felt it was presumptuous for a layman to try to teach when there were clergymen in the audience. Bible information on the Millennium Era is too sketchy for even a trained theologian to handle. Frankly, I was offended by your brassiness in tackling such a hazy and delicate subject."

The other New Zealanders standing around me were horrified at the priest's onslaught and began to melt away, one by one. Soon we were left standing alone in the center of the room, while the rest kept a courteous distance away.

I said, "Father, I simply don't know what to say. I'm so sorry to have offended you. My wife and I are only in your country in response to an invitation from New Zealanders to minister. Now, as regards this coming-Millennium message, I have spent almost a year doing prayerful research through the Bible on this age. The message was laced with scripture. I am very particular about accuracy. It grieves me that this has upset you so deeply."

Some ten minutes later I was asked to address the group. At this stage I was so deeply wounded the Lord had to carry on with no help from me. Only by His help was I able to minister at all. The response after the meeting, however, was encouraging. After greeting people individually we headed out to the parking lot. While driving back to the home of our hosts I began to share what Fr. John had done just before I spoke. We were baffled by the intensity of the priest's reaction to the Millennium teaching and started to pray as we rode along.

When it became my turn, I prayed along this line: "Dear Lord, thank you for this difficult experience. I know that all things work together for good. Please forgive me for my own bristling against his attack. But Lord, would you bring a troubling on Fr. John? Don't let him rest until this conflict is resolved. May there be a healing for his sake and for the cause of Christ. And would you somehow bring it about before we leave town? Thank you, Lord. Amen."

Our emotions were still pretty lacerated so, after having promised our hostess that we would be back in time for dinner, Virginia and I borrowed the car and headed for the seashore.

We walked along the beautiful New Zealand coast but soon found a restlessness rising within us. There wasn't the refreshing we had hoped for at the beach after all.

I said, "Honey, let's go on back. This walk isn't doing anything for me." Virginia agreed and we drove back through beautiful green hills studded with thousands of fleecy sheep. When we wheeled into the driveway our hostess came flying out to the car, with her finger at her lips.

She whispered, "Guess who's here. It's Fr. John. Can you believe it? I told him you wouldn't be back for a couple of hours but he insisted on waiting. He's there, pacing back and forth, in the living room.

I said, "Good grief! This must be why we felt such a tug to come back ahead of schedule. I guess we hadn't expected the Lord to answer our prayer so quickly. Can you stall him for a few minutes? I need to collect myself and pray before I can face him. What's his mood?"

She said, "I don't know, but he seems pretty uptight."

Some ten minutes later I decided to face the music and headed for the living room. My voice cracked nervously as I stuck my head in the doorway, waving feebly and said, "Good afternoon, Father. It's a surprise to see you here. Did you want to see me?"

After a cool greeting, he started an attack on the Millennium teaching. There came a strong sense to let him disgorge his hard feelings. The verbal barrage rose to a peak, but after a few minutes it was as though his "anger batteries" began to run dry. His final objections sputtered feebly to a stop.

I said, "Fr. John, present-day Christianity is indebted to your late Pope John. When he encouraged Roman Catholics to study their Bibles and allow the Holy Spirit to move it was like a fresh breeze blowing through a dank cathedral. Hundreds of vivacious Roman Catholics have encouraged me in various meetings around the world. Their contributions in praise and worship have been terrific. And their eagerness to believe that God is still a God of miracles has taught a lot of we Protestants something priceless."

The priest just stood there with a puzzled expression. Apparently he thought I was going to explode against his attacks on my message. It became obvious he was in the throes of inner conflict and finally he blurted out, "I am an arrogant man and I can't stand it anymore! You have been humiliated and abused by me. It was hard to come here today but there was a compulsion and I couldn't rest until I faced you. I was so agitated by what you had to say and now I'm so miserable. Would you pray for me?"

The change was so unexpected it staggered me for a few seconds. Then I walked slowly across the room and laid my hands on his shoulders and looked into his face. When I started to pray it was like a cloud lifted from us. I felt detached from the torrent of prayer coming from my own lips. The Lord was obviously with us and up to something.

The following half hour was gloriously mindblowing. Fr.

John wanted prayer and he got it. God's lightning had come to him! In vibrant sequence the magnificent priest (1) spoke aloud the sinner's prayer; (2) prayed for a healing of his bitterness; then capped it all by praying (3) for the power of the Holy Spirit. The thunder of God was at once beautiful and awesome! His prayers were answered with tears of joy. The troubled priest became gloriously electric!

A session of animated interchange followed. Finally I said, "Father, would you do something for me? I feel the Lord would be pleased if you'd lay hands on me before you go. There's a very heavy schedule before us here in New Zealand. Both Virginia and I would benefit by your prayers for us. Would you lay hands on me now and ask God's blessing? It would mean a lot to me, John."

His reaction was startling! In a swift recoiling motion, he stepped backward and said, "I can't pray like you do. No, no, I'm not worthy to lay hands on you! Please don't even suggest it."

Earlier the priest's intellect and his traditions had ganged up to create in him a terrible repulsion toward my teaching. A dark shadow had been cast in his mind over the realities of the Millennium Era. After just an hour together, the Lord had beautifully changed the priest from negative to a dynamic positive. But, now he imagined that I was too holy for him to pray over. He felt unworthy to even lay his hands on me. He had swung much, much too far the other way.

I knelt and took his wrists, placing his hands right on the top of my head and said, "Fr. John, I insist that you pray for me right now. I need God's blessing through your prayers — don't rob me of this by getting a false feeling of my own holiness."

Father John dutifully spoke a few hesitant words and then a great dam broke! The power and presence of God came into that room like a flood. Never have I experienced prayer that so shook my soul! The prayer went on and on, and on... four minutes... five minutes... eight minutes . . . Finally I was squirming down there on my knees. Muscle cramps were coming into my legs. I started to laugh softly as Fr. John thundered on in prayer . . . First I couldn't get this priest to start praying for me and now I couldn't get him to stop!

When I got up I was struck with the wonderful change in his countenance. I threw my arms around him and we both hopped around in a circle, laughing and crying. Never had I felt closer to any brother.

Now it was time for Fr. John to leave and we headed arm-in-arm toward the door. Just before he reached for the knob, he turned and put his hand on my shoulder. He said, "George, I'm seeing something." Staring up at the ceiling with a misty expression, "It's clear as real life, and it's wonderful."

I looked up at the ceiling and couldn't see anything. I asked, "What are you seeing, John? Tell me."

Fr. John said, "I see you and me sitting there on a big rock. It's the Millennium, and we're talking. I'm nudging you and saying, 'Here we are, and it's real!' You know, George, you were right about the Millennium after all!"

2

STRANGER THAN FICTION

It will blow your mind!

Those early streaks herald the approach of that Millennium Day and its brilliance defies description! "Eye hath not seen, nor ear heard, neither have entered into the heart of man, the things which God hath prepared for them that love Him" I Cor. 2.

Brace yourself as we run and skip through *MILLENNIUM MAN*. If the realities of Millennium life seem too good to be true, don't let them stagger you. We will be remade to withstand its glories: "But we all, with open face beholding as in a glass the glory of the Lord, are changed into the same image from glory to glory. . ." II Cor. 3.

If this account seems like a Jules Verne science-fiction fantasy, keep cool; TRUTH REALLY IS STRANGER THAN FICTION! "For my thoughts are not your thoughts, neither are your ways my ways, saith the Lord. For as the heavens are higher than the earth, so are my ways higher than your ways, and my thoughts than your thoughts" Isa. 55.

It's a strange paradox that enlightened 20th-Century man is so ill-informed about this looming age. Though we are now in the Space Age, many still hold such miniscule perspectives . . . Preoccupied with the sensual — the mere transitory, focusing on the things we can SEE, HEAR, TOUCH, SMELL and TASTE. The "me and my little world of the now."

Even so, deep inside there's a built-in KNOWING whereby most everyone has a sense of eternal existence, a subconscious realization that death is but a vehicle into another plateau of continuing life. The poet caught it —

> *Art is long and time is fleeting*
> *and the grave is not its goal; . . .*
> *Dust thou art to dust returnest*
> *was not spoken of the soul.*
>
> — Longfellow

The mere three score and ten of this phase of our existence is so tiny when compared with forever. What could be more relevant than to explore that future? So let's raise our vision far above natural horizons and, for one exciting hour, survey that Millennium Era.

Godly teachers have, in recent years, illuminated the two other pivotal events soon to occur: the "Rapture" (I Thess. 4:16,17) and the Tribulation Era. By now we have a pretty keen sense of both.

But why are we still so foggy-minded about the great age which immediately follows them? Millennium has always seemed so hazy, almost like a fairy tale, hasn't it? And we've tended to get it scrambled around in our thinking with Heaven and the Perfect Age. Have you ever wondered about the coming thousand year "Superworld"?

* What will we look like?
* Who all will be here during the Millennium?
* Will we see the past saints?
* What will be our relationship to the millions of non-Christians still alive after Armageddon?
* Will there be births and deaths?
* Will everyone be the same age?
* Will we just rest and harp?
* Will we ever visit other planets?
* What will our day-to-day life be like?

Sixty-four-dollar questions indeed! And by the time we have cruised on through the book these and scores of other Millennium questions will be answered for us.

Perhaps this dearth of Millennium teaching, 'til now, stems from a Divine strategy of timing. The Books of Daniel and The Revelation were unfathomable to those of prior generations — like so much meaningless gobbledy-gook; so puzzling and resistant to understanding. Yet, those past believers sensed their mysterious messages were deeply meaningful.

Why then was their content so hard to crack? The writings of God are often like coded messages — for believers only. Jesus' parables carried secrets for the privileged ears of His followers. They once asked Him, "Why speakest thou unto them in parables?" Jesus answered, "Because it is given unto you to know the mysteries of the kingdom of heaven, but to them it is not given" Matt. 13. And in I Cor. 2 we are told, "But the natural man receiveth not the things of the Spirit of God: for they are foolishness unto him: neither can he know them, because they are spiritually discerned."

Jesus described a myriad of conditions which would all impact during one particular generation. Looking down through the corridor of time, He saw those who would be alive when the curtain of this age would close. We are the generation Jesus saw and spoke about, and so, right on cue we are experiencing the death throes of the age.

So it's little wonder there is such an explosion of interest in end-time prophecies. Like a Divine kaleidoscope, ancient Scriptures are blazing out in new clarity. Even so, *Millennium Man's* secrets won't be understood by just anyone. "None of the wicked shall understand, but the wise shall understand" Dan. 12.

The Lord deposited scriptural veins of prophecy which are now being fulfilled before our eyes. What could better demonstrate that our world isn't some ship driven by winds of accident? Or better prove the Bible as hauntingly accurate? God laid prophecies like deposits of gold, then covered them for such an hour as this. He said, "Daniel, shut up the words, and seal the book, even to the time of the end" Dan. 12.

He then wrote clear instructions as to their uncovering in the proper day. "And in that day shall the deaf hear the words of the book, and the eyes of the blind shall see out of obscurity, and out of darkness" Isa. 29.

Why, of course! The time has now arrived for understanding of not only the "Rapture" and the Tribulation, but also of Millennial Life.

SECRET SHARING

Several weeks ago, a strong impression came into my thoughts. It went something like this: "Life is becoming increasingly complex as the present age stutters to a close. Believers will often know fear, discouragement, and even times of hopelessness. The remaining days will grow more treacherous, yet it is so very important that no believer falter just before reaching the prize of the high calling, that not one fall through despair, just a few feet — a few heartbeats, from the finish line.

"It is urgent that a clearer view of the glittering, Millennial prize be flashed on the screen of their understanding; to encourage and to steel believers, that none become castaways so close upon Millennium.

"Strengthen ye the weak hands, and confirm the feeble knees. Say to them that are of a fearful heart, be strong, fear not."   — Isa. 35

3

THE AGONY AND THE ECSTASY

His congregation roared when the preacher said, "I am trying to unscrew the inscrutable!" It was only half funny to me, for I could empathize. ... Little did I know, as the inspiration struck to write *MILLENNIUM MAN,* of the dragons I'd encounter down Manuscript Road.

Monsters of fear, futility and despair snarled at most every paragraph! Days and weeks blurred into months of pouring over Scripture. But the ongoing pursuit of its truths and realities was fueled for me by periodic scintillations as Millennium verses began to flash open their secrets.

The enormous potentialities of unveiling this coming age was compelling through the writing. Vision for the work was like a huge block of granite approached by a sculptor with chisel and hammer. Only he could see a Pieta buried in the massive rock. Could he ever unlock her? Such precision and delicacy would be necessary to avoid mutilating her substance while cleaving away the extraneous.

Had the sculptor also trembled as he approached the raw block? Oh yes, I'm sure he did.

But could the scope of Millennium ever be unveiled in our day? If ever it could, believers would never again be quite the same! Yet the task seemed overwhelming ... The Kingdom Age Scriptures are so strung out as to appear hopelessly entwined. Co-mingled with Heaven itself, the latter Perfect Age, natural kingdoms and the Kingdom of God within each believer. A kingdom within a kingdom.

Early one morning while laboring over the manuscript, a note sounded to write about the presence of God's glory during the new era. It was like a thunderclap! I immediately sensed this would change the whole planet's atmosphere from negative to positive. A glittering new aspect of Millennium life, and yet, how could THAT ever be expressed?

After hours of prayer and pondering I could still think of no way to describe this glory except by the word GLORY, itself. How do you describe the indescribable — the infinite?

With all of Gertrude Stein's eloquence, even she was semantically stifled, at times. In one moment of rhapsody, she struggled to share the mystery and the ecstasy of a rose. But, alas, it was just beyond her reach to write down what she had so clearly seen in her heart. Finally, in exasperation, Gertrude scrawled, "A rose, is a rose, is a rose. . . ."

The limitations of compassing supernatural truth while working with the crude tools of natural language can, at times, be painful! From time to time my head pounded as I stretched to paint an accurate word-picture of Millennium.

During one segment I paced the office floor in frustration trying to get something down on that Glory-of-God effect. Finally, after two days of writing, I was looking at fewer than 300 words. In disgust I cried, "Dear God, I am such a fool! Walking in here where theologians are too wise to tread. I'm so ignorant and so unproductive. Why, oh why is this book so hard?!"

Within seconds a response rang back through my mind. It was gentle, "Don't be too harsh with yourself. While on earth, didn't I know the trials of expressing the inexpressible? I too felt limited by the dimensions of natural language in transmitting the supernatural. Teaching intricate spiritual mysteries through parables: 'The kingdom of God is like . . .'

"My son, be comforted. It is now time to further open

Millennial truths — it is time to demythologize My coming Kingdom Age.

"It will be especially profitable for My own during these darkening hours before the dawn. I have written, 'In that day shall the deaf hear the words of the Book, and the eyes of the blind shall see out of obscurity, and out of darkness' Isa. 29."

". . . He shall guide you into all truth . . . He shall declare unto you the things that are to come."

4

THE EDGE OF TIME

One day Jesus sat with an intimate circle of His disciples while they asked about things to come. Man has long sought to pull back the curtain of tomorrow. Those close to Jesus felt at liberty to query Him about the future.

MILLENNIUM MAN will illuminate the prospects for our uncertain world by drawing on the only accurate Data Bank — the Source who controls the future. "The secret things belong unto the Lord our God: but those things which are revealed belong unto us and to our children forever" Deut. 29.

It's WHERE men turn for their information that counts. Millions of dollars are lost by people acting on tips from undependable sources about futures in such things as stocks and even the races. Faulty information can bring tragedy. Courts of law always gauge the reliability of their sources of evidence. So must we be sure of the trustworthiness of our own future's data — for on it hinges our destiny.

Millions of marriages have been destroyed by sheer gossip. Bloody wars have exploded when momentous decisions were made on faulty intelligence. It is a life-or-death matter that we heed THE BOOK in our own life decisions.

Millions are spent trying to get a look into the future through WRONG means, such as the occult. Pharoah wasn't the only politician who staffed his court with seers. Several present-day leaders are known to employ occult means in their governing processes. Some heads of corporations think it fashionable to inquire of "fortune tellers" to assist in their decision-making. Hundreds of thousands consult their horoscopes in daily newspapers. The consequences to humanity from these occult practices are often mental illness, bondage and even suicide. Dabbling in tomorrow can be a risky business for the universe.

Present-day fascination with the occult stems from man's quest to know future events before they happen, Satan, being the arch-opportunist, has played on this curiosity for 6000 years. The Tower of Babel was used for ancient astrological efforts. For this abomination, God fragmented humanity by confounding its speech.

In view of all this wreckage caused by future-seeking from forbidden sources, you would think man would wise up. But don't hold your breath.

King Saul couldn't wait to find out how the war he was fighting would turn out. During the night he stole out of camp to ask the Witch of Endor. Saul got an answer alright. Along with the occult revelation, severe judgment! The very next day a decapitated Saul hung by his heels — twirling in the sun. Saul gambled with his life for a peek into the future, and lost!

How foolish is man! When will he acknowledge the Bible as the perfect "fortune-telling" book? Does that shock you? Well, the semantics may shake us up, but let's face it, the Bible is the one and only dependable look into the future. With just this Book, any sincere person can accurately learn his own destiny — good or bad. Not just a few irrelevant tidbits from some crystal-ball gazer; not just a few bones from a seance. The Bible reveals mankind's entire panoramic future.

But why trust THAT Book The Bible has taken more ridicule from the academy than any book in history. It has been called sheer mythology, inaccurate and even foolish. But its message has proven indestructible. The more it's attacked, the greater it shines; hundreds of pages of history written in advance, nearly one-fifth prophetic.

The Bible is self-authenticating — archaeologists have been astounded by the accuracy of its record of past civilizations. Modern scholars acknowledge that it has often been ahead of science. Back when men said the world was flat, the Bible said, "God sits upon THE CIRCLE OF THE EARTH . . ." Isa. 40.

The Bible's history-written-in-advance has awed godly scholars by its perfect batting average. Most of the prophecies about men, cities and nations have already come to pass, exactly how and precisely when the Bible said they would. These events have marched right out of prophecy and into our history books. This majestic parade of prophetic fulfill-ment proves that humanity lives under a Divine management.

Yes, the Bible is an accurate Book of Fortune. So let's find out about our own future from the One who controls that future. "For the prophecy came not in old time by the will of man; but holy men of God spake as they were moved by THE HOLY GHOST" II Pet. 1.

Jesus foretold the circumstances we now see all about us. As we read the Bible's account of our day, it's like reading *Time* magazine. He wanted His followers to know when civilization had arrived at the edge of time. We are the generation about whom Jesus said "When all these things begin to come to pass then look up, for your redemption draweth nigh" Luke 21.

Before we travel into the world of the future let's synchronize our watches with the Great Clock in Heaven.

It's not easy to believe we're standing at the end of this age. Everything looks as though it will go on and on. Though our world is experiencing crises, shortages and discourage-ment, we are still getting along pretty well. We're still building, buying and marrying. Some say, "Hasn't the world always had problems?" Jesus said there would be those who wouldn't believe the end was near. But Christians can see these things through spiritual eyes.

Charles Duncombe wrote in *Christ for the Nations* magazine, "The signs of history's approaching climax are multiplying. A few years ago those of the academy predicted that the salvation of the human race would soon be achieved through the magic of man's mind. Their prophecies of Utopia have faded. Their bright pictures have been darkened by the clouds of pessimism and what one writer called 'irritated futility'.

"Each year closes with the usual parties, fireworks, whistles and bell ringing, but they sound out over our cities crippled with brown-outs and fuel shortages and sickened with crime.

"For the Christian, however, one magnificent and radiant star shines in the dark sky: He knows that these world pains are the birthpangs of a brand-new age which is about to be born. The hands once nailed to a cross are about to seize the reins of human government. We are now praying with added excitement, 'Thy Kingdom come'!"

Jesus saw how this present generation would face conditions similar to those before the great flood. God, through Noah, had warned the sin-mad people. For years Noah urged them to believe God and escape the coming judgment.

Noah pleaded with them to heed the Word of a compassionate God who desired that they repent and thereby survive the coming deluge. But they scoffed, branding old Noah a doomsday crackpot. They passed him off as a religious fanatic. The pre-flood philosophers, like many today, assured the people they needn't lose sleep over Noah's doomsday warnings. They went on doing their thing up to the first ominous drops . . .

Here we go again in the 20th Century! The Lord has prepared the "Ark of Salvation." He is calling earth people to enter in through His Son, the SS Salvation Captain, Jesus Christ.

Who will listen this time? Many more, I trust. But, again, millions are laughing at God's jet-age Noahs.

5

TOMORROW'S PAPER

Let's breeze through a few present clues which may help us see how close time has skidded to the edge. All the better to rejoice at the nearness of golden Millennium!

THE GENIUS CLUB

The membership of the Club of Rome consists of some of the world's distinguished thinkers and experts from many fields. Recently the C.O.R. undertook a penetrating study of mankind's odds for survival in view of five global threats: RUNAWAY POPULATION, ENVIRONMENT POISONING, DEPLETION OF ENERGY, RAW MATERIALS AND FOOD.

After inserting all exponential growth data on these into a computer, the C.O.R. experts concluded that Earth simply can't support its projected life in the near future. It shook the genius club!

ZERO POPULATION GROWTH

There are new unprecedented trends in humanity. Could the recent slowdown in baby production be another edge-of-time indicator? In the 6000 years since God said, "Be fruitful and multiply" (Gen. 9), there has been an acceleration of births. But now, many nations are approaching zero population growth. Statisticians say that within a matter of years there will be only one child to every four adults. Could this reduction in the number of babies be related to future world carnage? Innocent children would suffer horribly in the coming Armageddon. It's a thought. "Prove all things; hold fast that which is good" I Thess. 5.

CONVULSIVE CRISES

Economist Robert Heilbroner has just released an outstanding new book titled *An Inquiry Into the Human Prospect.* He writes, "The outlook for man is painful, difficult, perhaps desperate ... The answer to whether we can conceive of the future other than as a continuation of the darkness, cruelty and disorder of the past, seems to me to be no. ...."

Heilbroner sees insurmountable threats to human survival: *"Runaway population, obliterative war,* plus *exhaustion of the environment."* He believes the only curb in sight to be the Malthusian crises of famine and disease. He sees another disturbing prospect, "An approaching danger of under-developed countries shaking newly obtained atomic bombs in nuclear blackmail to secure massive redistribution of the world's wealth ... We now face convulsive change, forced upon us by breakdown and catastrophe wherein future survival is at stake and may be possible only under some SUPERGOVERNMENT capable of rallying obedience far more effectively than would be possible in a democratic setting."

Is the stage being set for a "supergovernment" to be headed by a brilliant world leader? Will he be the antichrist?

Prime Minister Spock of Belgium issued a statement that

further amplified the world's cries for some Super Statesman to surface. Spock is quoted as saying "The truth is that the method of international committees has failed. What we need is a PERSON, someone of the highest order, of great experience and great authority, of wide influence and of great energy. Let him come, and let him come quickly. Either a civilian or a military man — no matter what his personality — one who will cut all the red tape, shove out of the way the committees, wake up the people, and galvanize all governments into action. The man we need and for whom we wait will take charge .... Once more I say, it is not too late, but high time."

The Bible prophesies that antichrist will surface and he will perfectly fit Spock's description!

THE EDGE

Dr. Arnold Toynbee, the eminent British historian and philosopher says, "The world now stands on the edge of an abyss." Toynbee sees little prospect of humanity righting itself to avoid some kind of a cataclysmic crash.

Billy Graham says, "The world is now facing a crisis of such proportions that our whole civilization is threatened."

Yes, our world is groaning for rescue — holding its breath for some momentous happening. "For we know that the whole creation groaneth and travaileth in pain together until now" Rom. 8. There is great restlessness among the nations of the world — a jockeying for power. An especially macabre dance about the world's power button — the Middle East oil pools.

Humanity is now functioning with but a thin veneer of decency. People no longer blush at even the grossest sin. The world seems poised in expectancy of new troubles. Managing the affairs between the nations has become a virtual impossibility. Every institution created to promote international harmony has flopped. The frustrating impotency of the United Nations underscores the failure of man's best efforts. In the last days, "distress and perplexities of nations."

Angry masses all around the globe are highly ignitable! They seem itching to fight, to steal, and to destroy. Incendiary speeches of the revolutionaries and the terrorists inflame to violence and war. The Prince of this World is whipping our planet into death throe convulsions.

The thoughts of Chairman Mao inspire the violent slogan, "Power grows out of the barrel of a gun!" A $4 million ransom was recently paid out for a man kidnapped by Argentine terrorists. A grand total of $52 million has been extracted at gunpoint to enrich war chests of violent Argentine groups. New political kidnappings are breaking out everywhere like some dark plague. Skyjackings, terror and murder stalk the peoples of every nation. In California a long list has been found NAMING people marked for death or kidnapping by terrorist groups. No wonder the Bible said in the last days, men's hearts would fail them for fear.

A recent newspaper editorial revealed a direct correlation between alcohol consumption and the crisis climate. Breweries and drug peddlers are having a field day selling their reality-blurring potions here on Trouble Planet.

THE PALE HORSE

Five years ago, British author C.P. Snow wrote, "Perhaps in ten years, millions of people in the poor countries are going to starve to death before our eyes . . . We shall see them doing so upon our television sets. But how soon? How many? These are the most important questions in our world today."

When Snow sounded this apocalyptic warning, it was dismissed as unduly alarmist. But this year, Americans were shocked as TV cameras panned across thousands of animal carcasses in Africa. As if that weren't enough, the television screens were filled with thousands of hollow-eyed, bloated and starving people.

God's Book-of-Fortune foretold famine galloping through the earth. "And I looked, and behold a pale horse; and his name that sat on him was Death, and Hell followed with him. And power was given unto them over the fourth part of the earth, to kill with sword, and with hunger, and with death, and with the beasts of the earth" Rev. 6.

Suddenly the world is experiencing shortage upon shortage — of things we have always taken for granted; gasoline, electricity, water, metals, food, wood, paper, plastics, etc. The list grows ever more ominous. Mother Earth has put up with so much from us. We have polluted her, sucked her treasures and abused her in ten thousand ways. She has given life and nourishment to her billions of heaven-defying passengers. But, a time of reckoning is fast coming. Earth needs and will soon get her Millennium overhaul.

"The night is far spent, the day is at hand, let us therefore cast off the works of darkness, and let us put on the armor of light" Rom. 13.

Present realities depress the drifting masses of today. But to each believer, they are Bible prophecies tolling an end to world corruption and joyously ringing-in that rapturous day! Good news is in the wind . . .

"For the Lord himself shall descend from heaven with a shout, with the voice of the archangel, and with the trump of God! Then we which are alive and remain shall be caught up together with them in the clouds, to meet the Lord in the air; and so shall we ever be with the Lord." — I Thess. 4

6

HAPPINESS IS . . .

Through this present life, flashes of pure JOY are like rare diamonds, experienced only intermittently — The first bird of Spring — Walking hand-in-hand with the one you love — A sunset — Christmas morning.

Life in the end-time is no picnic. Too often we find ourselves trudging through days strewn with problems. Sometimes it's cause for celebration just to make it through one. The carefree times are too infrequent.

But why? It's like labor pains — time groaning to give birth to a magnificent Millennium — "creation waits eagerly for the revealing of the sons of God ... For we know that the whole creation groans and suffers the pains of childbirth together until now" Rom. 8, NAS.

So, "Hang tough — we've almost got it made." Let's not falter when we're about to break out of this 6000-year "Firefight" into a dazzling Millennium world. All those things that wear us to a frazzle are just about doomed. I pray Millennium's realities will so explode in you that the cares of this present time will pale — that discouragements can never again take root. Only a God-kind of truth has that explosive capacity!

Time is a brutal taskmaster — Living by the sweat of the brow is a drag. Besides, "We battle not against flesh and blood, but against spiritual principalities and powers."

Little wonder the fearful blur with booze. Pep pills to wake them up, tranquilizers to float them through the day, sleeping pills to knock them out at night. Much in life has been a tough proposition. But, hold on, our wild ride through time is about to translate itself, like some drab caterpillar, into a dazzling butterfly!

Twentieth-century man feverishly works at the pursuit of happiness but often ends up with only a hangover. Plastic happiness is big business, while true happiness eludes his grasp.

But for the believer it's just the opposite — HAPPINESS is pursuing him. And that happiness will win out for the Hounds of Heaven are swifter than the Hounds of Hell. The warm breezes of the Millennium Age are about to fill the earth. What a day!

Satan fouled Eden and gained temporary earth domin- ion. Since then mankind has struggled in an uptight world. Never having experienced anything else, it's difficult for us to imagine the exhilaration we are about to feel as all this is changed.

The moment Satan's evil is shorted out, streams of laughter and deep joy will follow. Beauty for ashes — perhaps those incandescent sunsets have been trying to whisper this secret.

Those nagging feelings of restlessness will vanish. Here- tofore we have sensed dissatisfaction even during moments of highest pleasure. An indefinable "something" is always missing. That long-awaited vacation, the anticipated moment of bliss — ALMOST perfect; — do you know what I mean? We will remain incomplete until we are with HIM. It's Jesus who will bring forth the full spectrum of life and He's coming soon!

We've been living constantly with pressures; and it will be that way until Satan is clobbered. He is the father of anxiety, guilt, loneliness, fear, jealousy, nervousness, hopeless- ness, pain, disappointment, sadness and hate. These devastating powers will, very soon, be brushed into oblivion. The broom of Jesus will sweep them into Hell, along with their inventor. Can you stand that kind of a change?

Will you miss the bill collectors? — the hourly reports from Bad News Broadcasting Company? — the smog — the surgeon's knife — the bloody wars — the screaming politicians — the cancer — the fat — the funerals? It will take a lot of getting used to, but I think we can make the adjustment, don't you?

You had better get ready to live in a brand new kind of world. God has designed one up there on His heavenly drafting board and it's just for us.

We can glimpse His "better idea for living" by examining the Garden of Eden prototype. We are nearing a renaissance of that Edenic magnificence, a restoration of that kind of world. It begins immediately following Armageddon's fury. How good to be on-the-in, knowing we are in a fixed fight and our side wins! Every believer has a stake in that Armageddon victory and will reap full beneifts from this cosmic victory for 1000 years!

When the last doomsday bullet falls back to earth, the New Age curtain will be drawn! Millennium life's hallmarks will be laughter, contentment, purpose, exhilaration, righteousness, peace, ecstasy and explosive joy!

The true and exotic nature of Millennium life might be labeled "HANDLE WITH CARE." It is Jesus' presence on our planet which lights, powers and beautifies Millennium. Yes, handle with care, lest we long for its benefits more than its Benefactor. The real focus of Millennium life will and must ever be the PERSON of Jesus, not the PLACE. JESUS is Millennium's architect, its centerpiece, its all. . . .

"Seek ye first the KINGDOM OF GOD and HIS RIGHTEOUSNESS and all these things shall be added unto you."

7

THE FRAGRANCE OF GOD

Millennium is going to be mighty exciting — like distilled lightning! So don't count on lulling around too long harping on your own pink cloud. That always seemed a bit insipid anyhow. There won't be any chance for the new life to get boring; it's going to be filled with assignments, challenge, fun and great purpose.

Satan looked like the winner when Jesus hung bloody and lifeless up there on Golgotha. The devil's kingdom must have celebrated wildly, crying "Victory at last!" — but their gloating smirks froze when, three days later, resurrection power bolted through the universe, raising up Jesus. Lucifer had played his trump card and lost!

Just as Christ was able to survive Satan's powerful blows, so shall it be with us. Ever since Jesus conquered Satan, we believers have been equipped for triumph in spiritual warfare. Christians are the gem-like remnant sifted from humanity who have, one by one, chosen to follow the Jesus they have never seen.

Believers who, through this Jesus, ran life's gauntlet of temptation, crises and pain, only to emerge with the prize of immortality. Like a radiant cluster of stars ready for presentation to the Heavenly Father, as proof of redeemable creation. Later to be whisked a million light-years away to glittering corners of the universe as a proud display. Jesus' victory trophies!

It is difficult to imagine any other kind of life, here on this angry planet. We've never known what it's like to live in a tension-free, harmonious world.

Each day Satan is loose, a discordancy permeates life. "... the whole creation ... travaileth in pain together" Rom. 8. Most of the animals which were intended to provide enjoyment, food and help have turned against us. The bear, the lion, the shark, all deadly! We live in fear of one another. Present life is run through a corridor of struggles, rampaging nature, wars, work and diseases.

Finally, as time and the frictions of life wear us down, we run in fear of DEATH! In this present era of earth's travail, even the birds sing with a hint of sorrow. Listen carefully — Do you hear that plaintive strain? Imagine the new Millennium sounds when captivity is taken captive and when travail has fled before Triumph.

Angry growls of the beasts will turn to purrs and new companionship. Laughter and contentment will be the fruits of new creation bliss. At last, "Peace on earth, goodwill toward men."

It's going to melt our hearts when we hear all creation tuned-up and praising God in full concert! Would you believe the hills and the trees actually joining our chorus? "... the mountains and the hills shall break forth before you into singing and all the trees of the field shall clap their hands" Isa. 55.

You can almost see the clear waters, brilliant skies, singing hills, exploding greenery and brilliant Millennium flowers. No more choking weeds; no devouring insects; no more killing droughts.

We will hear the pleasant sounds of progress. The whole tempo of the universe will become melodic — "... let the heavens rejoice, and let the earth be glad; let the sea roar, and the fullness thereof. Let the field be joyful, and all that is therein: then shall all the trees of the wood rejoice" Psa. 96.

Millennium — the titanic fulfillment of Jesus' 1900-year prayer, "Our Father which art in heaven, hallowed be Thy

Name, Thy Kingdom come, Thy will be done on earth, as it is in heaven." Can't you sense its nearness?

Recently, I visited a beautiful lake village in Northern California. In my first meeting I told the gathering about a reaction when I first arrived: "Most of you know I live in Los Angeles. During my first hour in Lakeport I was mystified by a peculiar "something" in the air. You people are used to it but a stranger can immediately smell it. I suppose we've all discovered that our own home has a distinctive odor, all its own. We seem to adjust to its smell; never noticing it until we've been gone for a while.

"Some of you have suffered the 'fragrance' of cities like Gary, Los Angeles and Pittsburgh. Or maybe some town with a stockyard upwind. Haven't you wondered how the people who have to live there stand it?"

By this time everybody was leaning forward in their seats, wondering what awful smell I detected in their town. I said, "You know, it took me an hour to identify the peculiar essence brooding over your whole area. Then, at last, I recognized the long-forgotten odor I was smelling — CLEAN!" They laughed with relief — but the little joke had a built-in truth.

By now the whole earth has a rotten atmosphere that would seem unbearable if we hadn't been forced to adjust to it. Do you know that sin stinks? That old serpent and all his demon helpers have a smell to their works. For example, there's a dank, ugly smell to nightclubs. It's a mixture of stale, rotten wine, tobacco and EVIL. We could bottle it under the label "Eau de Sin" but I don't think it would sell too well. Then there's the stench of Satan-induced cancer, gangrene and vomit; the smell of hospitals.

Sin, rot and death emanate odors mindful of the "foul Spirits" Jesus spoke about. Since earthlings have never lived in an atmosphere free from human and demonic pollution — brace yourself — you are going to have an overwhelming and glorious reaction to Millennium's fragrance!

Did you know God has a delicate sense of smell? He

speaks often of frankincense, spices, the sweet-scented trees and the flowers of Lebanon. We catch a hint of God's character exuding from His lovely flower blossoms. Sensing the person of Jesus, the Psalmist wrote, "All Thy garments smell of myrrh, and aloes, and cassia" Psa. 45.

Every one of our five senses will be intensified at the moment of our translation. New fragrance will strike our whole being like an exquisite musical chord!

HIGH VOLTAGE!

When we are sick or just plain tired, nothing much feels, tastes, looks, smells or sounds good. But when we are rested, healthy and happy all our senses take on new dimensions. We say, "Everything seems rosy." Imagine the "high voltage" of our new Millennium senses. Only then will we know what REAL LIVING is all about!

When immortality surges through us it will quicken with a bolt of resurrection life. We will pulse with new vitality and infinite new capacities to savor God's people, angels and His all. The body is "sown in weakness: it is raised in POWER" I Cor. 15. Jesus power!

We will throb with pleasant new energies. We will want to skip and explore His creation. Get ready for a life of full-spectrum gusto in Millennium. That "mortality might be swallowed up of life."

8

PLOWING THE EARTH

This present age will depart with a roaring crescendo but there's a glorious purpose through it all — A colossal global facelift! Everything evil and rebellious must be "plowed up." The Tribulation days will be brutalizing, particularly in the final part when Satan rampages and God responds with a doomsday intensity.

"The GREAT DAY OF THE LORD is near, it is near, and hasteth greatly . . . the mighty man shall cry there bitterly. That day is a day of wrath . . . a day of darkness and gloominess, a day of clouds and thick darkness . . . And I will bring distress upon men . . . because they have sinned against the Lord . . . Neither their silver nor their gold shall be able to deliver them in the day of the Lord's wrath" Zeph. 1.

Everything still defiant in human civilization is going to feel the rain of 100-pound hailstones, fires, falling stars, pestilence, famine and tormenting creatures sprung from hell! This dying age will mercifully expire with Armageddon while hundreds of millions are fighting along a huge battleline ranging from Turkey to the Arabian peninsula. The plains of Megiddo churn like an angry sea from a rain of doomsday bombs and bullets. Blood, flesh and fire fill the air! So devastating, it will require months just to burn the weapons and bury the bodies.

"For they shall burn the weapons with fire . . . and they

shall sever out men of continual employment, passing through the land to bury" Ezek. 39.

At the height of Tribulation's devastating earthquakes many of today's Sodom-like cities will be pulverized into sand. The Richter scale will hit 10 as whole islands flee away. New land masses will convulse upward out of the waters. Gigantic mountain ranges will redistribute their substance in staccato heaves — The whole planet lurches under multiplexing energies and forces suddenly unleashed. Skyscrapers, cities, ships, planes and many people are obliterated. Fires rage through the world —

Can the planet stand anymore?

"For, behold, the day cometh, that shall burn as an oven; and all the proud, yes, and all that do wickedly, shall be stubble: and the day that cometh shall burn them up, saith the Lord of hosts, that it shall leave them neither root nor branch" Mal. 4. But keep in mind it's a wise God bringing LIFE to His beautiful master plan for humanity.

A beer commercial was aired over and over again for many months. Most of us heard the jingle, "YOU ONLY GO 'ROUND *ONCE* IN LIFE SO GRAB ALL THE GUSTO YOU CAN!"

I'm afraid we have a little bad news for them — it won't be quite that simple ... All the "gusto grabbers" who have rejected Jesus and gone 'round once in life will be shocked to find themselves in a "second go'round," facing the living God!

Oh how they'll wish they could have only gone 'round once and then just disappeared. But, no way. Every person will eventually stand before God. "It is appointed unto men once to die, but after THIS THE JUDGMENT!"

DAY OF THE LIBERTARIANS

Some may say, "But I thought all that Tribulation carnage was going to be caused by Satan and the antichrist." That's not the whole picture. Satan's reign does have its own big day under antichrist alright. He puts on a show, that all may see what it's like to live with unrestrained evil. Tribulation people who experience this licentiousness are going to learn, the hard way, what it costs to dance to Satan's tune!

Three and one-half years into the Tribulation, antichrist is assassinated! But he is "resurrected" by the False Prophet. At that instant, Satan utterly possesses antichrist. From this moment on all pretense of benevolence stops; Satan "takes off his gloves" — but so does God! The 3½ years that follow become the last round of a winner-take-all fight. Satan "empties hell's arsenal" in a desperate frenzy to retain control over earth. But Satan's 6000-year lease is broken and Christ repossesses the world through the power of His might.

But you may say, "Why, oh why, mess up the whole planet in this fight?" There is a reason. God is very efficient; everything He does has a symphony of purpose. He is usually accomplishing many things with one stroke. So it is with these catastrophic years before Millennium dawn. . . .

From all those bursts of earthquake-energy, not only will earth receive a facelift, but also newly increased land surface to provide more living area. "Every valley shall be exalted, and every mountain and hill shall be made low: and the crooked shall be made straight, and the rough places plain" Isa. 40.

Today it's fashionable to undertake urban renewal projects. Have you ever watched the rebuilding process? First the wrecking crews: Swarms of bulldozers, wrecking balls and dynamite reduce old, decaying structures to rubble. Along come the builders who "magically" erect handsome, new facilities. Presto! The area is "born again."

So it will be with this tired and abused planet. Physical earth also needs to be "born again." But before it can, there must be a clearing away of everything decadent. Our all-wise Heavenly Father knows He must "PLOW UP THE EARTH," root out and eliminate everything that won't harmonize with His Millennial-life blueprint.

Through those earthquakes He will redistribute the waters and the lands — all within days. "And there were voices, and thunders, and lightnings; and there was a great earthquake. . . . And every island fled away, and the mountains were not found" Rev. 16. Great firmament rearrangements which will both enhance the cosmetics of the planet and provide vast, new habitable land area. There is, presently, an enormous 140-million-square-mile land area hiding under our oceans. These "land masses" include mountains higher than Everest and chasms deeper than the Grand Canyon. Realms to provide the most pleasant scenery.

All present faults and strains will be relieved during that series of exploding quakes. When the dust settles, our planet will be entirely earthquake-free. "Behold, the Lord maketh the earth empty, and maketh it waste, and turneth it upside down, and scattereth abroad the inhabitants thereof" Isa. 24.

It may also be that the 22° tilt and the earth's wobble will be corrected by the finger of God at the same time. These may have been caused by the violence in Lucifer's rebellion. Meteorologists say these irregularities contribute to the climate extremes: hurricanes, floods, blizzards, droughts, etc.

When her tilt and wobble are corrected, we will see an idealizing of earth's climate. "And I will cause the shower to come down in his season; there shall be showers of blessing. And the tree of the field shall yield her fruit" Ezek. 34. And through Isaiah, "And the parched ground shall become a pool, and thirsty land springs of water; in the habitation of dragons, where each lay, shall be grass with reeds and rushes" Chapt. 35.

DAY OF THE ROGUES

"The Son of man shall send forth his angels, and they shall gather out of his kingdom all things that offend, and them which do iniquity" Matt. 13.

When I used to think of these years of chaos, my

suspicious mind visualized a random annihilation of the people unfortunate enough to be alive. But God will see that great care is exercised in this vital end-time sorting. The Death Angels will be under very tight rein. (Read Matt. 13.) There is nothing "chancy" in God's character.

Often, through history, God has moved under a Divine principle of screening out the righteous before a great judgment begins — Noah's family, before the flood; Lot, before Sodom's obliteration.

Another such time involved Ezekiel who, by the Spirit, was lifted up between the earth and the heaven and while there he was shown a vision of this Godly principle in action. This is what Ezekiel saw:

The city of Jerusalem had become the scene of many abominations. God described it as "a land full of blood and a city full of perverseness." Because of this wickedness, the Lord called out six men with slaughter weapons and one man with a writer's inkhorn.

He said to the man with the inkhorn, ". . . Go through the midst of the city, through the midst of Jerusalem, and set a mark upon the foreheads of the men that sigh and that cry for all the abominations that be done in the midst thereof" Ezek. 9.

After the "mark of God" had been placed on the forehead of each person whom God saw hated unrighteousness, a final order was given to the slayers, "Slay utterly old and young, both maids and little children, and women: but come not near any man upon whom is the mark; and begin at my sanctuary." It is sobering that God started with the church people. He always deals with those of His own household first.

QUALITY CONTROL

God will carefully read the heart of each person during those last-chance tribulation years. Those whom He sees have potential to harmonize with the upcoming Jesus' reign will be spared. "Say unto them, As I live, saith the Lord God, I have no pleasure in the death of the wicked; but that the wicked turn from his way and live: turn ye, turn ye from your evil ways; for why will ye die" Ezek. 33. Those who turn to the living God will gain favor and salvation. "and a book of remembrance was written before Him for them that feared the Lord, and that thought upon His name. And they shall be Mine, saith the Lord of Hosts, in that day when I make up My jewels; and I WILL SPARE THEM . . ." Mal. 3.

But all the rest whose hearts irreversibly harden toward God, must be screened out. Many will have given themselves over to lasciviousness, rebellion and violence and been found to be irretrievable. These will be marked as "rogue humans." They probably wouldn't like Millennium life nor heaven either, for that matter. Hell will better suit their style since they shall, of their own accord, have chosen against God.

God is never whimsical; His sorting of humanity will be loving and deliberate. "And He shall separate them one from another, as a shepherd divideth his sheep from the goats . . . Then shall the King say unto them on his right hand, Come, YE BLESSED of my Father, INHERIT THE KINGDOM prepared for you from the foundation of the world" Matt. 25.

His inspection plan bears the cutting edge of truth, doesn't it? A loving Heavenly Father WILL separate for Himself a people who can blend with one another throughout the polished reaches of eternity . . . .

MILLENNIUM MYSTIQUE

Millennial life is an era of great purpose; a season when the work of earth's rehabilitation must be accomplished. First, Armageddon, then: TO WORK! There will be limited time for "harping," — Praise God! Earth will be plowed and ready for our loving attention. Ready to be replanted, rebuilt and reorganized.

Modern Israel is a striking type of the restoration work that must be done in the earth during Millennium.

The Lord granted Abraham a title in perpetuity to the territory which includes present-day Israel. After centuries of putting up with Jewish defiance, God temporarily drove them from their own land. During their absence, and while under alien stewardship, the land grew barren and desolate. Stripped of trees, untilled and unwatered, promised land became wasteland. Finally, the Jews returned to their devastated inheritance.

By now Israel has been restored; under God's blessing, AND BY THE WORK OF THEIR OWN HANDS. The Bible foretold how this land would, through restoration, become so transfigured that visitors would exclaim, "It looks like the Garden of Eden!" This has come to pass in our day. (See Ezek. 36:35.)

The Jews are being gathered from the four corners of the world; a dramatic fulfillment of prophecy. Similarly, the Bible tells how, at the close of Armageddon, the Jews and all righteous Gentiles will again be gathered up, under God's direction.

Yes, the Millennium rebuilding will be accomplished, both through supernatural acts and by human endeavor. We can look forward to thrilling months, witnessing changes in this exquisite planet, while it is being restored to its Edenic perfection.

Millennium citizenry will include all of the saints, plus the millions of unsaved people still alive at the conclusion of Armageddon. The entire society will be directed from Jerusalem, the world's capitol, and headed by Jesus, King of the earth. He will delegate authority and power to the saints who will reign over designated areas under Him. "And he said unto him, Well done, thou good servant; because thou hast been faithful in a very little, have thou authority over ten cities" Luke 19. Millennium won't be a classless society, but one with well-defined orders allowing a high order of efficiency under our Lord's direction.

Are you exhausted already; — just thinking about your assignments during the Millennium? Never, never will it be tiring, but instead it will be a stimulating time with the vitality of immortality pulsing in every cell. Our knowledge, wisdom and ability will have been instantly expanded at the moment of our translation. We will have "the mind of Christ." Never again to experience mental sluggishness or forgetfulness — the dynamic of resurrection power ours at last. Complex problems will then become very simple. Assignments will then be easy for us. The joyful sounds of progress will grace the Millennium years. What a day!

The Lord descended from above,
And bowed the heavens most high,
And underneath His feet He cast
The darkness of the sky.

On cherubim and seraphim
Full royally He rode,
And on the wings of mighty winds
Came flying all abroad.

He sat serene upon the floods,
Their fury to restrain;
And He, as sovereign Lord and King,
For evermore shall reign.

— Psalm paraphrase
by Thomas Sternhold

9

SCIENTIFIC SAGA

During the Millennium science and technology will reach a stratospheric zenith! In recent years, many Christians have imagined scientific progress was totally at odds with the spiritual. Perhaps this misconception arose because some in the academic world are avid attackers of God's Word. Certain campuses have become hotbeds of anti-God teaching. When science and technology began to peak, a trend developed to exalt the creature more than the Creator. "Thus saith the Lord, thy redeemer, and he that formed thee from the womb, I am the Lord that maketh all things; that stretcheth forth the heavens alone; that spreadeth abroad the earth by myself" Isa. 44.

The Bible foresaw our present-day scientific advances: "knowledge shall be increased" Dan. 12. But, Satan tirelessly works to pervert every good thing. He fans the tendency to beat the breast and cry, "I am the master of my fate and the captain of my soul!", thus encouraging man to become cocky about his accomplishments. During the space triumphs a near worship of science arose. The prince of this world will use anything (even science) to divert worship away from God.

Man has never, in the full sense of the word, created anything. That's a pretty strong statement, but a true one. Science and technology merely apply existing laws of nature and work with already existing materials.

But, there's been a giant leap both in technology and

science since the turn of this century. We have seen a cascade of startling developments: The telephone, radio, automobile, airplane, atomic energy, laser, computer, television and space flight.

Have these great achievements forever angered God and violated man's relationship to Him? Why, of course not! Men are working with His elements and energies already placed here. It was the Lord who commanded man to "subdue the earth" and who said, "Do whatsoever you do with all your might as unto Me."

It was God who designed and created the incredible human brain and He who put us here to rule the planet. Imagine what a colossal civilization we would now be enjoying if Adam hadn't allowed mind-polluting sin to deteriorate the human species. Sin has obstructed the full flow of human progress.

But do you realize how many great scientific break-throughs have occurred through God's inspiration of scientists? Only from the perspective of eternity will we discover the extent of Divine inspiration behind many modern achievements. There are countless testimonies of super-naturally inspired inventions among Christians working in the field of science. A host of great men openly credit God for scientific insights following prayer.

This shouldn't come as a surprise. In James we read, "If you lack wisdom, ask of God, and He will give it liberally" Chap. 1. Most of us have, at one time or another, felt Divine inspiration. If satanic inspiration can move the medium and the murderer, then Godly inspiration can direct a Christian engineer.

DR. RODNEY JOHNSON of the National Aeronautics and Space Administration is a modern-day "for instance." He has told of his years at General Electric when the Lunar Excursion Module (LEM) was under development. The LEM was essential to the Apollo Program as the final critical space link to transport the astronauts down to the surface of the moon. After the astronaut's work on the hostile moon surface was completed, the LEM would then have to be capable of flying the men back up for a precision rendezvous with the command ship.

The intricate LEM would have to be extremely light and compact, able to be carried on the long journey to the moon. It would have to incorporate great power, reliability and maneuverability to fulfill its delicate space role. The exotic vehicle had to incorporate full life-support systems for its crew and also serve as a space truck; carrying the tools, test equipment and even a lunar car. The space link would then have to provide constant communication to the mother ship and incorporate fail-safe redocking features.

These design requirements were "impossible"! We all became so fascinated with the powerful booster rockets and the Apollo command ship, that we overlooked the stupendous challenge of the Lunar Excursion Module.

Dr. Johnson tells of the agonizing mental strain that went into the LEM's development. Its designers faced a maze of engineering obstacles — they were pushing far beyond the present state-of-the-art. At virtually every point they needed components, electronics and materials that didn't even exist.

Dr. Johnson and several other Christian engineers prayed each morning, before work. Before picking up a slide rule or punching a computer button, they gathered and prayed for wisdom. Slowly, these technical barriers started to fall in response to their barrages of prayer. Dr. Johnson attributes the LEM's brilliant success to their partnership with God, in its conception.

Space great, Dr. Werner von Braun, has also acknowledged God's role in the space program. There are many others.

HALL OF FAME

JOHANNES KEPLER was a brilliant German theoretician who worked closely with the foremost astronomers of his day. He unlocked the secret of the planets' paths, discovering how they move in elipses. The science of astronomy is grounded on Kepler's laws of planetary motion.

Johannes Kepler was a fervent, praying Christian, as well as an authentic genius. Some years ago his personal work logs were found, and a learned team of scholars was hastily assembled to translate his material for inclusion in modern science textbooks. The translators were baffled as they struggled with the great physicist's brilliant material — they couldn't tell whether his work was religious or scientific. Kepler would write in his work log a paragraph of intricate equations, then alternate with a paragraph of praises to the Lord! No wonder God shared great cosmic mysteries with Kepler.

MICHAEL FARADAY was a physicist without peer. The electrical measurement, the FARAD is named after this eminent and classic physicist. For 20 years he interspersed his brilliant scientific achievements with the preaching of the Gospel — every single Sunday!

SIR ISAAC NEWTON formulated the law of gravity — that masses attract each other with a force directly proportional to weight and inversely proportional to the square of the distance apart. It is to Sir Isaac we owe the familiar, "to every action there is an equal and opposite reaction." Newton also built the first reflecting telescope and discovered that a prism separates light into its component colors. But, first and foremost, Isaac Newton was a fervent disciple of Jesus Christ.

THE FEARSOME GENIE

But what is mankind's principle gain through the recent explosion of knowledge? TROUBLE, that's what! But, why? TROUBLE, because man is sinful, selfish and at enmity with his Creator. In our present vulnerable state, many great scientific achievements have been turned right back to harm mankind. Man's scientific growth has outraced his moral character.

Today, at the very pinnacle of scientific attainment, our planet is wracked with violence, disease, hunger and hate. Chemical advances have given us not only medicine and wonder materials, but LSD and napalm!

The invention of motion pictures was an immediate delight to man. Before long, however, films began to spread unspeakable moral pollution by glorifying their violence, perversion and filth.

Yes, we have abused the fruits of science. It was a treacherous thing to let the scientific genie out of the bottle while man was still so in league with evil. Ever since the first murder, by Cain, sinful man has feverishly worked to invent better and better slaughtering tools. One breakthrough after another vested temporary advantage to its inventors. It has been so from the crossbow to the atom bomb!

The two great world powers are spending $100 billion every year to gain military advantage, one over the other. Too much of man's "subduing of the earth" is now centered in the scientific disciplines of warfare. The "Genie" has already created enough destructive power to enable man to blast his own planet off its axis!

Yes, it's true, scientific discoveries in themselves don't offend God, but their perverse usage does. These incredible disciplines will find outlet for the blessing of humanity when, at Millennium's dawn, "They shall beat their swords into plowshares, and their spears into pruninghooks . . . neither shall they learn war any more" Isa. 2.

What a day! Come quickly, Lord Jesus . . .

10

SUPERMIND

*Thought and speech are God's gift to man,
intimately associated with Him and
impossible without Him.*

— A.W. Tozer

The mind is an astounding creation. It's a maze of intricate circuitry, linking some 20 billion neurons and 160 billion glial cells. A super-computer which could not be duplicated, even with acres of the most advanced present-day, high-speed, electronic computers. Imagine the human brain: 180 billion parts smoothly linked and silently powered by electrochemistry. The entire wondrous machine neatly housed in a small bone-protected sphere. The ultimate in microminiaturization! If there was nothing else by which to glimpse the incredible brilliance of God, the human brain would do.

Neurosurgeons and behavioral science researchers say the incredible human brain is now functioning at less than 7% of its design capacity. This loss of mental efficiency stems directly from the fall of man through sin. Since we have seen such brilliant accomplishments, while using only a fraction of the brain, imagine what will be done when unshackled Millennium minds are turned loose in science and technology.

Arthur Longley has brilliantly comprehended the electrifying surge of new mental energy believers will soon experience: "We ought to make it perfectly clear that immortality is not a rest-cure for nervous wrecks in a parkland rehabilitation center, 50 billion miles away, but instead it is God's practical scheme to reshape civilization for the common good of mankind. Suddenly, at the Rapture, the Christian will inherit life force that will stimulate the brain to high levels of intelligence, capable of grappling with the problems that now baffle the world's greatest minds."

There will be other stimulants to the new civilization. The literal residency of Jesus on the planet will infuse new vitality into all human endeavor. And, it is no small thing that the massive scientific efforts now concentrating on weapons research can then be directed toward the blessing of humanity.

It is not difficult to forecast presently unimaginable benefits accruing to Millennium civilization as a result of new teams of ultra-brilliant minds focusing on constructive developments. Millennium think-power will get a further boost as a result of the mind's being coupled with vibrantly healthy bodies. The human being is a complex system with its sub-systems interrelating. For example a weak, diseased body hampers the efficiency of the mind. Fear, tensions and sickness war against the perfect operation of the mind. When sin is banished the mind will blossom. Sin effects our mental engine like sand effects gears.

There will be phenomenal consequences from this sudden unshackling of human creativity. "The spirit of wisdom and understanding . . . the spirit of knowledge . . . shall make him quick of understanding" Isa. 11. This touch in our minds will bring giant leaps in the fields of communication, transportation, energy and agriculture. Shall we consider a few of these exciting possibilities?

The world is now troubled by near exhaustion of the petroleum supply — less than a 29-year reserve. Many are worrying what we earthlings will do to fuel our cars, trains, ships, airplanes and electric generating stations. Statisticians gloomily foresee lights, wheels and engines sputtering to a stop. But we have a Creator whose schedules and timetables are always precision-perfect! Before all of earth's gears lock up for want of lubrication, this age will close. The oil supplies which God placed in the planet will prove adequate to squeak through this era.

Then Millennium technical breakthroughs will provide the new "Superworld" with inexhaustible, pollution-free energy alternatives. A glass of water has more energy locked into its molecular structures than we get from a million barrels of oil or from 100 thousand tons of coal. Matter is energy-packed and we will see it unlocked to provide unlimited pollution-free power.

Millennium engineers will be capable of bringing us many fascinating benefits. Pocket-size picture phones which will allow us to dial anybody in the world. Even today, with our satellite links, instant global communications are possible, using bulky installations similar to the transceivers in Air Force One. During the past 30 years brilliant progress has been attained in the electronic field, using only a fraction of the human mind potential. So, it's certain we can anticipate a Millennium scientific explosion!

The technology of the new age, with its atomic engines and magnetic power, will provide efficient, clean, silent propulsion. The ecologists would love Millennium. Millennium will, at last, see an ecological utopia.

MILLENNIUM MAGIC CARPETS

Congestion, accidents and pollution are consequences of our overcrowded streets and groaning transportation systems. Twentieth-century man still travels almost exclusively in one highly congested plane — the earth's surface. This will be corrected. Even with the thousands of planes now flying, our skies are virtually unused. There are hundreds of additional transportation corridors in the air above us.

Riding public supersonic airbuses or our own nifty aircars, we will be traveling these airways. This will enable Millennium man to swiftly and effortlessly go anywhere. We will see new engines, super-metallurgy, tiny computers, advanced navigation satellites, laser landers and revolutionized aerodynamics. Fast and easy to fly vehicles will be as easy to build as our mass-produced automobiles.

It isn't difficult to visualize a six-passenger supersonic aircar that would be "driven" as easily as we now pilot our own cars. With automated flight controls and landing systems, it will be possible to dial Peking for lunch, and — click, click, be on our way! Even today automatic landings are becoming common occurrences. Millennium aircars will hover and land effortlessly, for parking in our own garage.

Beautiful air freighters, perhaps a mile long, computer-directed through their own assigned air corridors. They will move fresh food, materials, and even houses; playing their part in ideal logistics and distribution for all of the Kingdom civilization.

Today's scenery is marred by millions of ugly telephone poles and power transmission lines. Millennium cosmetics will neither tolerate nor require such crude interconnecting systems. Every building will have its own compact power unit built in, to supply all its needs. Likewise, there will be no phones or other communications systems which are not completely wireless.

We Millenniumites will carry our own pocket T.V. We won't want to miss the stream of news from World Capitol, Jerusalem! With these pocket portables we can watch the breathtaking Millennial transformations taking place around the world. "Behold, all things become new" — and right before our eyes!

Good news will be a hallmark of the age. The present "Bad News" broadcasting networks will be out of business.

Perhaps newscasts from other parts of the universe will be one of the exciting Kingdom Age features. New interest in the wholesome will replace the present macabre fascination with evil and violent news. No longer will men have such an appetite for the works of darkness. Won't it be nifty to get newscasts devoid of war, famine, murder, rape, robbery, riots, hate and nerve-wracking politicians? But those telecasts will crackle with exciting good news!

MEMORY MIRACLE

Flawless memories will be characteristic of the Millennial mind. Won't that be a neat bonus? How often we have yearned to remember people's names! Then we will instantly recognize one another — even the saints from past generations, "but then shall I know even as also I am known" I Cor. 14. Won't it be something to talk to new/old friends like Noah, Peter, Jonathan and David? Just like Peter instantly knew Moses and Elijah on the Mount of Transfiguration. (See Luke 9) and how great to chat with more new friends like Martin Luther and those "no name" Colosseum heroes.

No more time wasted hunting lost items. Never again to forget important facts or lessons. No more "blanks" in our mind.

BABEL REVERSED

Another exciting Millennium change will bring great joy and new efficiency to mankind during the Millennium — a new language. According to Wycliff there are 5,698 different known languages in the world today. What a terrible toll, in frustration and misunderstanding, these thousands of tongues have caused mankind! God sent this confusion of tongues upon mankind as judgment for Babel (see Gen. 11). But, He

has also promised "I will turn to the people a PURE
LANGUAGE that they may all call upon the name of the
Lord, to serve Him WITH ONE CONSENT" Zeph. 3. Can
you hear everybody praising Jesus in the same language, at
last?

THE TIME MUSEUM

From the moment man is born he has to wage a running
fight with sickness and death. Particularly for those now
battling pain, the coming glory holds special promise. Instant
renewal of aching and aging bodies is imminent and it can't
come too soon. There is a weariness among the peoples of
earth. ". . . they that wait upon the Lord shall renew their
strength, . . . they shall run and not be weary, . . . walk and
not faint" Isa. 40. And for those fighting the ancient enemy
of sickness there is striking good news: "the Lord Jesus
Christ, who shall CHANGE OUR LOWLY BODY that it may
be fashioned like His glorious body." The ULTIMATE in
healing!

Yes, sickness and pain will be smashed for every
Millennium saint. "The eyes of the blind shall be opened, and
the ears of the deaf shall be unstopped. Then shall the lame
man leap as an hart, and the tongue of the dumb sing"
Isa. 35. Vibrant physical and emotional health will be the
Kingdom Age norm! And Millennium's perfect moral and
spiritual environment will insure against any relapse. Immortality is a forever state!

We should ever bear in mind the "two-tiered" Millennium society. Many benefits each glorified saint will enjoy
won't be available to the non-glorified populace. For example, there will be death, aging and probably sickness
among those who haven't exchanged corruption for incorruption.

Maybe there will be a Time Museum with displays of all

those obsolete things like hearing aids, toupees, dental drills, eye glasses, surgical tools, wheel chairs and crutches. All these could remind us of the glory of our new estate. Every stress, heartache and pain now encountered by the born-again Christian will flee on Millennium morning. "I reckon that the sufferings of this present time are not worthy to be compared with the glory which shall be revealed in us" Rom. 8.

11

MISSION CONTROL

The Bible makes it clear that Jesus chose to work, during His 33 remarkable earth-years, as the Son of MAN. He dramatically proved what a sin-free MAN can accomplish while acting in harmony with God. Jesus boldly divested Himself of Divine advantages and functioned in the same sin-charged environment we know.

But if Jesus worked as the Son of MAN, how did He perform all those miracles? Rebuking storms, raising the dead, walking on water, multiplying bread? And how did the MAN-Jesus know about the woman at the well's past life?

Jesus has freely told His secret but men are unwilling to pay the price to do as He did. But the opportunity is still open to us.

What were His victory secrets? Jesus never allowed the world's sin-drenched environment to overcome Him. Yet Jesus experienced the same temptations we do. This purity kept the "hot-line" to His Father wide open. Did you ever before realize that there is POWER in purity? Yes, there's power in purity and obedience. There is no dynamic in ascetism but only in a godly, genuine righteousness. Because of Jesus' perfect obedience and His perfect holiness there was an unbroken power line to all resources of the Father.

Jesus often said, "All that I do, the Father showed me." By disciplining every earthly impulse and acting in harmony with the Father, Jesus retained the constant backing of

Heaven. No wonder He was able to do such mighty works, even though here as the Son of Man.

Several weeks ago Russ Busby, the photographer for World-Wide Pictures, was shooting stills at Pat Boone's home in Beverly Hills. After the picture session was over, Russ, Pat and I drifted into a very stimulating discussion about this relationship between Jesus and His Father.

During the Apollo project the world saw a beautiful working harmony between Mission Control and the astronauts. All of the intricate tasks done by the astronauts on these missions had been learned in their pre-flight training sessions at the Houston Space Center. Mission Control was constantly available for guidance during their efforts out in space, and the communication link between the astronauts and the center was absolutely essential to every mission success.

The astronauts were constantly backed by all resources at Mission Control. The training, the backing, the obedience of the astronauts and their instant "hot line" to the space center made possible the string of breath-taking space successes!

So it was with Jesus. During His work down here on the planet earth Jesus, too, was continuously backed by heavenly "Mission Control" with all its wisdom, resources and unlimited power.

By maintaining purity in His life and thereby a constant access to the power of Heaven, Jesus moved victoriously, even in the midst of this world's sin environment. No wonder He performed such incredible feats!

This victory formula will work for us too. We, too, qualify for that instant backing of the Father. "That whatsoever ye shall ask of the Father in My name, He may give it you" John 15. Through prayer, we too can call on the same "Mission Control" resources Jesus tapped. When operating in harmony with God's Word, Christians are able to see a fulfillment of Jesus' startling promise, "greater things shall ye do."

LATENT POWER OF THE MIND

Jesus' mind is also worthy of our attention and we who walk in the Spirit, "Have the mind of Chirst." That is a staggering truth!

Looking back from the perspective of eternity we may be amazed to learn how much Jesus accomplished through having His then-mortal mind smoothly harnessed with the Holy Spirit. Jesus' keen insights into people and situations were possible through the combination of His mind functioning at full potential and blended with the Spirit.

Our computer-like brains are now partially "shorted-out" by SIN. Similar to the way man-made computers are disabled by acid shorting out the electronics. Everyone has experienced, sometime, the effect on their own thinking powers when sin enters. Confusion, poor judgment, etc.

Worry and fear, as a result of sin, markedly affect our minds. The brain is also affected by guilt when it is burdened with unconfessed sin.

Over 50 thousand violent deaths occur each year as a result of the impaired mental abilities of drunk drivers. Drugs and alcohol wreak havoc in the brain's delicate "circuitry."

Since all corruption will have been put off from the glorified saints, we can see how the transformation in the Millennium mind will enable fantastic mental accomplishments. New harmony with God will likewise bring an indescribable sense of well-being far exceeding the most delightful state of mind we have ever known.

Vibrant harmony between spirit, mind and body will explode into colossal accomplishments and joy. Oh, the ecstasy of unbroken communication with our Lord!

". . . and reaching forward to what lies ahead, I press on toward the mark of God in Christ Jesus"
— Phil. 3

12

FOUNTAIN OF YOUTH

I suppose each of us has wondered what we, personally, will look like in the new age. Every year spent in this sin-impregnated world has been brutalizing. Every earth day grinds at our being like a sandstorm tearing at a flower.

At one time or another, we've all peered into a mirror to examine time's relentless work . . . tick, tick, tick. Here a deepening wrinkle, there another little strain line. Remember the mini-crisis of spotting a first gray hair? While ever so subtly the eyes slip their focus. Later, the unwelcome weariness too early in the evening . . . tick, tick, tick.

The wages of time is irreversible death to the physical. Death starts its work the day we are born. Billions are spent each year by people trying to fight off old Tyrant Time. But, alas, we can only powder, patch and dye for a season. Soon the Geritol and the cosmetics fail before time's terrible engine.

Men have paid heavily in their search for some elusive fountain of youth, Elixers, super-drugs, diets and plastic surgery. Anything to fight back that relentless ticking clock. But time has never yet been denied her pay!

Let's face it; wouldn't we all like to find the fountain of youth? This deep yearning to find eternal life and to defy aging has inspired a lot of fancy fiction. A recent TV series, "The Six Million Dollar Man" is about a man who was marvelously rebuilt after a "fatal" accident. Suddenly, he's able to outrace horses, leap over buildings, etc. Behind all the smoke of fantasy, could there be some real fire of immortality — a true fountain of youth somewhere? Here, again, truth will soon outrace fiction.

When the believers' clock strikes "RAPTURE," Lookout! A real fountain of youth, at last! Paul wrote, "We ourselves groan within ourselves, waiting for the adoption, that is, the REDEMPTION OF THE BODY" Rom. 8. Our fountain of youth will prove to be TRANSLATION, through Jesus. Live reality will soon transcend cold theology!

Have you been looking in that mirror and felt depressed by what you see? Then change to Jesus' mirror, "But we all, with open face beholding as in a glass the glory of the Lord, are changed into the same image from glory to glory, even as by the Spirit of the Lord" II Cor. 3. So don't let the enemy ever again lay a spirit of despondency on you because of those little aging marks. Look in God's mirror and rejoice!

Say, "Pride of Life, out with you! Any hour now I'll be plunged into Jesus' fountain of youth! And I'm not coming out as just some retread, but better, much better than ever!" "Who shall change our vile body, that it may be fashioned LIKE UNTO HIS GLORIOUS BODY" Phil. 3.

No more wrinkle cream, no more glasses, no more girdles, no more Clearasil, no more crutches, no more diets and no more pills! Never again to know insomnia, fear, pain or disappointment. Let's hear it for Him. "Hurrah for Jesus!"

But what will you look like? Will you be completely different? Yes, you will be different and yet, somehow more YOU than ever! Brace yourself — you're going to like the real you! "There is a natural body, and there is a spiritual body . . . And as we have borne the image of the earthy, we shall also bear the image of the heavenly" I Cor. 15.

Will you be recognizable to your friends? On the Mount of Transfiguration, Peter instantly recognized the glorified Jesus, though there was a great supernatural glow — a heavenly quality that emanated from His being.

When he saw Elijah and Moses talking with Jesus, Peter immediately knew both of them. Later on, when two of Jesus' disciples walked along the road to Emmaus with the resurrected Christ, He looked to them like a man. When Mary saw Jesus outside the tomb, He didn't look like a spectre, but a real person, and He was.

After resurrection, Jesus led many back from Hades and right into the streets of Jerusalem for a short while. ". . . And came out of the graves after His resurrection, and went into the holy city, and appeared unto many" Mat. 27. A nostalgic detour on their way to Heaven.

In another incident, after the resurrection, Jesus suddenly appeared among the disciples. He invited Thomas to touch and to handle, saying, "Behold My hands and My feet, that it is I myself; handle Me, and see; for a spirit hath not flesh and bones, as ye see Me have" Luke 24. Immediately, Thomas answered, "My Lord and my God!" John 20. The resurrected Jesus also participated in a Galilee fish fry.

But the new Jesus also had some marked differences after the resurrection, didn't He? He was still able to function in earth's natural environment but could also, at will, transcend it. He was no longer constrained by either gravity or matter. Jesus could appear in a room without coming through the door. Just as a television signal is freely able to move right through the whirling atoms of solid-appearing materials, so it will be with us after our own translation. The disciples watched as Jesus "ignored" the pull of gravity when, from the Mount of Olives, He soared upward like a beautiful, silent missile.

Earlier, Jesus had demonstrated His ability to move into Hades itself. No force, no matter, no being could restrain His actions. Jesus was given all power in heaven and in earth. It is His will that we share this as joint heirs with Him.

Believers are promised, "We shall be LIKE HIM." Are you beginning to grasp the wonder of it? "Behold, I show you a mystery . . . we shall all be CHANGED, in a moment, in the twinkling of an eye . . . for the trumpet shall sound . . .

and we shall be CHANGED" I Cor. 15. David caught this magnificence when he wrote, "I shall be satisfied when I awake with THY LIKENESS" Psa. 17.

STRATIFIED SOCIETY

The millions of non-glorified Millennium citizens won't be either a physical or a mental match for the saints. If they were to compete in such competition as sports or even chess, they would be no match. These would have to be separate leagues. The saints would embarrass the fabled "Six Million Dollar Man" in any task — physical or mental.

But those "ordinary" Millenniumites will still experience great bonuses from the new era: There will be longer life. "There shall be no more thence an infant of days, nor an old man that hath not filled his days; for the child shall die an hundred years old" Isa. 65.

Back in the Old Testament times there was elongation of life. Abraham fathered Isaac when he was past 100. Moses' vital life forces were still bright when he was 120. In still earlier times, before Satan had so fully polluted humanity with sin, people lived still longer. Children were born to 700 year-old parents.

During Millennium, there will be three pluses for the non-glorified over that Methuselah Era of longevity: (1) Jesus will be present on earth. (2) Satan will be totally out of business (3) No wicked people will be allowed to corrupt society.

In Millennium, good-bye and good riddance to all the forces that decay the flesh, depress the brain, and shackle the human spirit. That will leave but one more enemy loose and death, too, will be forever conquered at Millennium's end.

Are you beginning to see how neat our Millennium is going to be? Some have erroneously imagined it as a sort of ethereal and idle vacation. That would give us the thousand-year "blah's." It's going to be a delightfully purposeful time!

Millennium children born among the unsaved populace will never have known anything other than its "hothouse" spiritual climate. They must each be tested for obedience and allegiance before they will be allowed to enter the golden eternity which follows.

Back in Moses' day, he challenged all the people, "I have set before thee this day life and good, and death and evil" Deut. 30. At some stage Millennium children will each have to make their own choice. God will make certain none enter the final Perfect Age who harbor the potential for spiritual rebellion. The short season of Satan's loosing, at the end of Millennium, will allow one last screening of all humanity. Each will get one last chance to choose good or evil. Final exams before our graduation into eternity!

Until they could be tested, Adam and Eve were denied access to the incredible tree of life. With an assist from the Serpent, they "blew it" and were ejected from Eden lest they eat of that eternal-life tree. God knew that, as a consequence of the fall, they would grow more and more evil and dare not be permitted to live forever. Otherwise they would have, through the centuries, developed into grotesque, reprobate beings.

But Millennium Christians who have passed this same test through Jesus WILL be invited to eat of that same great tree. "To him that overcometh will I give to eat of the tree of life, which is in the midst of the paradise of God" Rev. 2.

In the process of our own translation, every physical flaw and sickness will go "poof"! "Then the eyes of the blind shall be opened, and the ears of the deaf shall be unstopped" Isa. 35. We will be touched instantaneously, both mentally and physically. All flaws resulting from sin, environment and heredity will be forever erased by our loving Heavenly Father. "It is sown in corruption: it is raised in incorruption: It is sown in dishonour; it is raised in glory: it is sown in weakness; it is raised in power" I Cor. 15.

The design of humankind is the most luxurious in all of God's creation. The "Rolls Royce" of His beings. Only PEOPLE bear the Divine stamp "Made In Our Image." We are fashioned to have the character qualities of none less than the Father, the Son and the Holy Spirit.

At translation, we will become what God originally intended. And that's important, since we will live in our new state forever and forever. "Who shall change our vile body, that it may be fashioned like unto His glorious body" Phil. 3.

Each believer will be a perfect and unique individual in the family of God. We will, at last, reach full stature and beauty as a one-of-a-kind person. The variety in all His creation is beyond human concept. Every snowflake, every fingerprint, and every person is different. God has no duplicates — no redundancy. He has but one YOU in all of His inventory. No wonder He has gone to such extreme measures to redeem each person.

So, it won't be long now until you'll be able to meet the person Jesus intended you to be. In a "twinkling of an eye," recast into the perfect, original design He worked out for you before even the world was fashioned. "He hath chosen us in Him before the foundation of the world . . . Eph. 1. And God never designed a homely, crippled or blemished person. He doesn't even know how to make "seconds." Each Millennium saint will be PERFECT and strikingly beautiful!

INSTANT "CHICKS"!

Have you ever looked at a group of senior citizens and tried to imagine what they looked like when they were younger? Won't it be fun, after translation, to see some of the lovely "young women" we've always thought of as old ladies?

Yes, Millennium saints will be vivacious and handsome! And this startling event will occur sometime soon: When He comes back He will take these dying bodies of ours and

Fountain of Youth 79

change them into GLORIOUS bodies like His own" Phil. 3, L.B.. It seems almost too good to be true, doesn't it? Since this is now approaching "Current Event" status, it might be profitable to look at it a bit closer.

At some coming microsecond of time (in the twinkling of an eye) glorified saints will find themselves far better than in their finest prime years — with throbbing beauty, vitality and freshness! We will, however, still carry into glorification, the accumulation of character values which we developed; — but not the painful negatives from this life.

YOUR BLUEPRINT

Physical imperfections aren't God's handiwork, but a result of accumulations from the thousands of years of human sin. These flaws won't be brought into the immortalized being.

The recreation of millions seems impossible, doesn't it? How could God ever be able to recast every dead and living saint into the perfect, prime-of-life persons He originally designed? How could He remember? Perhaps there is a clue.

Within each cell of our body is a chromosome. Buried within the DNA bases of the nucleus of each cell is a mysterious chemical code, sometimes called the *hereditary code.* I like to think of this as our own personal blueprint. Stamped within this amazing *hereditary code* are the features, size, coloring — every minute detail of your person.

A copy of your own blueprint is secure in "heaven's files." It will be a small thing for our big God to instantly remake us to the original, perfect design from our own hereditary code blueprint. So, in that microsecond, at translation, you will be recreated to God's Divine specifications. Now we can see why there is no need to fret about aging or physical imperfections. They are but temporary nuisances.

With this cellular blueprint we can also see how God can perfectly recreate the millions of past believers whose bodies have been decayed, burned or lost at sea. Isn't that wonderful?

A THOUSAND-YEARS YOUNG

The built-in capacity of the human body to replace its own cells is utterly fascinating. This remarkable ability for self-repair may hint at Millennium's eternal-youth capability. Most cells of our body can replace themselves when injured or worn. This automatic cellular replacement will be perfected in Millennium. You can see how a 1000-year-old could easily retain "glowing youth." A continual renewing of our every cell.

The Lord has, at times, even caused inanimate objects to retain their newness. During the 40-year desert trek, the Jew's clothing and even their shoes never wore out. An exciting picture of God's capacity to keep our person eternally shiny, new and vibrant! Surely He can do for our bodies what He has already done with inanimate shoes. And we'll want that eternal vitality. There are a billion galaxies to visit and a lot of forever to enjoy.

13

THE TIME MACHINE

To prevent total genocide, Jesus will, at the peak of Armaggedon's fury, take captivity captive. Its guns will be spiked and Antichrist and False Prophet thrown into the lake of fire (see Rev. 20). Satan is forcibly chained and imprisoned. Immediately following the lock-up ceremony, every earthling who survived Armageddon will go through a moral and spiritual "X-raying." And there will be no hiding place in all the world for the fleeing wicked. This all takes place during a day of strange twilight. "And it shall come to pass in that day, that the light shall not be clear, nor dark: But it shall come to pass, that at evening time it shall be light" Zech. 14.

Strong angels will track the wicked to their most remote hideaways. Every single person who is spiritually incurable will be denied entrance to the Millennium. The Lord will block evil, corrupt humans from infecting or tormenting believers in the new age.

Reprobates will have sealed their own fate by resisting Christ's salvation during this lifetime. "Men loved darkness rather than light, because their deeds were evil" John 3. And, ". . . who knowing the judgment of God, that they which commit such things are worthy of death, not only do the same, but have pleasure in them that do them" Rom. 1. Their sick joke, "Jesus saves — TRADING STAMPS!" will burn in many ears for eternity.

There is precedent for a Divine elimination of hopeless incorrigibles: The priests of Baal were destroyed on Mt. Carmel for contending with God's prophet, Elijah. Corrupted Sodomites were dispatched in one blinding flash! Attention, Gay Libbers!

Ezekiel plainly saw God's repulsion toward unrighteousness in a prophetic vision when God ordered the man with an inkhorn to "set a mark upon the foreheads of the (righteous) men that . . . cry for all the abominations that be done in the midst thereof." Immediately after all of the righteous people had been duly marked by God's man-with-the-inkhorn, He spoke again. This time six slayers were given their orders, "And to the others (the unrighteous) He said in mine hearing, Go ye after him through the city, and smite: let not your eye spare, neither have ye pity: Slay utterly . . . but come not near any man upon whom is the mark; AND BEGIN AT MY SANCTUARY" Ezek. 9.

God's attitude toward evil, which is so starkly outlined in that vision may, at first, seem harsh, but instead it reveals what He MUST DO to prevent the wicked from again corrupting Millennial civilization. His post-Armaggedon inspection will start with the Church — with a spiritual "X-raying" of His own household first.

There is another account in the New Testament which reveals the shock of certain persons who, when they "approached the Kingdom of Heaven" were told, "I never knew you; depart from Me, ye that work iniquity" Matt. 7. The only key that will work the golden tumblers of Heaven's lock is righteousness — THROUGH Jesus Christ.

Why, of course! How could a Holy God spend an eternity with the unrighteous, even though they had done mighty works in the sight of men? They had futilely sputtered, "Lord, Lord, have we not prophesied in Thy name? . . .and in Thy name done many wonderful works?" The day is fast-approaching when each of us must approach heaven's door! Do you have that one and only Jesus-key? Hurry, there's still time to get it!

Today we hear so much "God is love" talk. Sure, He's a God of LOVE, but it's essential to remember He's also a God of JUSTICE. No plastic, counterfeit religionists are going to make it through heaven's door. Jesus accurately said, "I am the Way, the Truth, and the Life: no man cometh unto the Father but by Me" John 14. The Jesus-key is the only one which can ever gain access to the Father.

For centuries Christians have feared the dread mark of the beast (666). But old Satan is just a counterfeiter — a cheap imitator. JESUS will be the mark on every believer, as his pass to eternity. "And His name shall be in their foreheads" Rev. 22.

THY KINGDOM COME

Once through Millennium Gate, no more nightmares, insomnia, anxiety, confusion, disappointment or fear. No longer that old false accuser causing painful memory flashbacks. God will erase harmful memories of those dark events from our past. ". . . and God shall wipe away all tears from their eyes" Rev. 7. Isn't that great? We couldn't have "joy unspeakable and full of glory" if our sorrowful memories were dragged along into the new age.

With the demon beings doing a thousand-year jail stretch there won't be anyone to operate the "factories of hell." Millennium saints will experience a sudden shortage of cancer, leprosy, diabetes, arthritis, toothaches, polio, V.D., insanity, worry, senility and funerals. Think you can get used to it?

Then picture all those OUT OF BUSINESS signs on the liquor stores, asylums, prisons, porno publishers, gun factories, distilleries, psychiatrists' offices, strip joints and clock factories.

"What's that — did you say clock factories?" Yes, I believe the glorified saints will have little need for clocks, watches and calendars. The Bible tells how a great angel will stand, with one foot on the sea and another on the land, to declare, "there should be time no longer" Rev. 10. Although this scripture speaks of a judgment delay, it also suggests still another exciting Millennium bonus. Perhaps you can sell that Elgin stock. We won't have too much use for their little time-machines during the Kingdom Age.

COSMIC SYNCHRONIZATION

What a slave driver TIME has been! How great it would be to just pitch out our jangling alarm clocks and never again be driven by tyrant time.

One day I was thinking about the implications of a no-clock Millennium, and it seemed mass confusion would surely result. Though clocks are terrible little task-masters they have been essential to coordinate our civilization.

TIME — I hate it, but even so, I really couldn't operate without it. How could we ever possibly do without our watch during the Millennium? The Lord began to show me a few things about time itself. Jesus' name, Alpha and Omega, reveals that He is the originator and perpetuator of time. He has precise awareness of events, progress and fulfillment. He charts the course and rhythms of the universe. Yet Jesus can never be pressured by the feeble ticking of man's little time-machines.

I said, "But Lord, how could Millennium believers ever function without watches? How would we ever keep appointments? Wouldn't there be rank confusion without our clocks?"

He reminded me of a personal episode I had completely forgotten. "Remember that trip when you forgot your travel alarm and you prayed to be awakened at six-thirty?"

I said, "Yes, Lord, I do remember!" I had been astonished when I turned on the light in my Dallas hotel room to find it was exactly six-thirty!

He said, "I answered that prayer by effecting just one of

the benefits of the coming age. During this present life, everything on earth suffers from disharmony with the rest of My creation. The rhythms in space, where sin has never touched, are still run with sheer perfection. The finest chronometers mankind has ever built are inadequate to measure the precision of their orbits. Every star and galaxy moves with fine geometric grace. Do I ever bring the sun up late? Yet I own no clock.

"Clocks serve mankind as a temporary crutch. They are essential while nature is in disarray through sin — and out of synchronization with the rest of My universe.

"In the instant of the believer's translation, every scar from the curse will be healed — you will then find yourself in perfect harmony with all creation. Suddenly you will KNOW what time it is! Everyone has experienced instances of sensing the correct time without the benefit of a clock. When you put on immortality this quality will be perfected in you. Then you will always know exactly what time it is."

Why, of course, for then we will KNOW as Jesus knows. No one can picture Jesus peering at a wristwatch.

And so, it will be "no sweat" to function most efficiently in the coming age even without those pesky clocks. We will then KNOW what to do and WHEN to do it through our new oneness with Him. The silky smoothness and harmony of Millennium society will be enhanced by this Divine "Super Time."

That in the ages to come He might show the exceeding riches of His grace in His kindness toward us through Christ Jesus.

— Ephesians 2

14

UNIVERSITY OF MYSTERIES

Lod Airport is big! She conveniently lies between Jerusalem and the sprawling city of Tel Aviv. Lod has a complex of runways and facilities which enables her to handle most of Israel's commercial and military air traffic.

In the coming age this great airport won't be able to handle even a fraction of the global visitors. Jerusalem will by then be the all-purpose capitol of the world (Rev. 21; Zech. 14). Into her will stream multitudes of joyous people by the airways, sea lanes and highways.

Millennium Jerusalem will be situated on a high plateau and she will become a very big city. The prophetic scriptures speak of a "coming up" to the city. "And it shall come to pass in the last days, that the mountain of the Lord's house shall be established in the top of the mountains, and shall be exalted above the hills; and all nations shall flow unto it" Isa. 2.

Jerusalem will become a river-side city. The very moment Jesus steps onto the Mount of Olives, it will split and a magnificent new river will flow out in either direction.

"And His feet shall stand in that day upon the Mount of Olives, which is before Jerusalem on the east, and the Mount of Olives shall cleave in the midst thereof toward the east and toward the west, and there shall be a very great valley; and half of the mountain shall remove toward the north, and half of it toward the south ... And it shall be in that day, that living waters shall go out from Jerusalem; half of them toward the former sea, and half of them toward the hinder sea" Zech. 14.

From the Talmud we catch a hint of the dazzling beauty of the Millennial-Era city. "Ten parts of beauty were allotted the world at large; out of these Jerusalem assumed nine measures and the rest of the world but one."

Looking through prophetic eyes toward Millennial Jerusalem, Jeremiah wrote, "Therefore they shall come and sing in the height of Zion, and shall flow together to the goodness of the Lord" Chap. 31. And Isaiah, who almost sang his inspired view of the jubilant influx, wrote: "Therefore the redeemed of the Lord shall return, and come with singing unto Zion; and everlasting joy shall be upon their head: they shall obtain gladness and joy; and sorrow and mourning shall flee away" Isa. 51.

In that day, Jerusalem will be THE PLACE to go. "And I will pour upon the house of David, and upon the inhabitants of Jerusalem, the spirit of grace and of supplications" Zech. 12. World action will be centered in Jerusalem and each year it will be our privilege to visit that City of Blessings. "And I will make them and the places round about MY HILL a blessing; and I will cause the shower to come down in his season; there shall be showers of blessing" Ezek. 34.

There's an interesting aspect to those yearly trips to Jerusalem during the Kingdom Era. Although traffic in and out of the Holy City will be enormous, Jesus will keep track of any who neglect to come. It will be His strong desire that each person visit Jerusalem every year and there is going to be a little penalty for shirkers:

"And it shall come to pass that everyone that is left of all the nations which came against Jerusalem shall even go up from year to year to worship the King, the Lord of hosts ... whoso will not come up of all the families of the earth unto Jerusalem to worship the King, the Lord of hosts, even upon them SHALL BE NO RAIN" Zech. 14.

All manner of people will flow into the beautiful city. Some will be coming to worship at the great Millennium temple which Jesus, Himself, will build. "And He shall build the temple of the Lord: Even He shall build the temple of the Lord; and He shall bear the glory, and shall sit and rule upon His throne; and He shall be a priest upon His throne" Zech. 6. Then again we hear of this same new temple, through the prophet Ezekiel: "And I will set my sanctuary in the midst of them for evermore" Chap. 37.

Others in the stream of Jerusalem-bound travelers will be coming to transact administrative affairs of the new worldwide government. It will be a very efficient administration with believers holding the KEY posts. "And he that overcometh, and keepeth my works unto the end, to him will I give power over the nations: AND HE SHALL RULE THEM" Rev. 2. And again in Rev. 20, "They shall be priests of God and of Christ, and shall reign with Him a thousand years."

There will be just one supreme political and spiritual Leader of the whole world. This era will see an end of present society's fragmentation because of diverse religions, languages, regimes and political systems. "And the LORD shall be King over ALL THE EARTH: in that day shall there be one Lord" Zech. 14.

LAW AND ORDER

We are in a frightening hour when justice is mocked. Many judges are weak and our courts are a shambles. Too frequently the guilty go unpunished. The court calendars are glutted. Justice has not only become slow but frighteningly uncertain. Truth has become elastic and as a consequence our civilization is reeling.

But Millennium justice will be a blend of harmony,

authority and fairness never before experienced in the earth. "Of the increase of His government and peace there shall be no end, upon the throne of David, and upon His kingdom, to order it, and to establish it WITH JUDGMENT AND WITH JUSTICE" Isa. 9. Then again through Isaiah we read of this dispensing of pure justice, "He shall bring forth judgment unto truth. He shall not fail nor be discouraged, till He have set judgment in the earth: and the isles shall wait for His law" Chap. 42.

Jesus' rule will banish earth's bloody warring, "And He shall judge among the nations, and shall rebuke many people: and they shall beat their swords into plowshares, and their spears into pruninghooks: nation shall not lift up sword against nation, neither shall they learn war any more" Isa. 2.

In the finest sense, Jerusalem will also become Fun City! "The voice of joy, and the voice of gladness, the voice of the bridegroom, and the voice of the bride, the voice of them that shall say, Praise the Lord of hosts" Jer. 33. Yes, Millennial Jerusalem will ring with laughter, excitement, dancing and purpose. It will be electrifying just to enter her gates!

CAMPUS NEWS

Some of the Jerusalem visitors will be coming as students to study at "JESUS UNIVERSITY" . . . "And let us go up to the MOUNTAIN OF THE LORD . . . and HE WILL TEACH US OF HIS WAYS" Micah 4. Isaiah wrote of those mind-enriching courses: "And all Thy children shall be TAUGHT OF THE LORD" Chap. 54.

Can you picture us strolling across the Jerusalem campus of "Jesus U" heading for our classes? Maybe we'll be taking course like:

Planet Management
Secrets of the Universe

Divine Principles
Celestial Music
Animal Management
Universal Laws
Cosmic Energy
Celestial Travel
Galaxy Pioneering

Yes, it could be. I always grumbled about going to school, but I can hardly wait to enroll in those classes where the Lord will be sharing deep secrets with us. By then we will have proven trustworthy to receive a first-hand unlocking of many of His great mysteries.

Because we will be joint-heirs and rulers with Jesus for eternity, such knowledge is essential for us to carry out our designated assignments.

But the Lord doesn't want us to coast in our present spiritual state, waiting for "Jesus U" classes. We have been exhorted to hit our studies hard while in this present life. "Study to show thyself approved unto God, a workman that needeth not to be ashamed, rightly dividing the word of truth" II Tim. 2.

So we should accelerate our intake of the Word in the time left in this age. There is a Divine principle whereby those who have "grown in grace and the knowledge of Him," are the very ones to whom He reveals still more. It isn't feasible to crash suddenly into the totally unfamiliar. What we KNOW by that time can serve as a bridge over which to reach further treasures of his UNKNOWN!

Yes, the Millennium will provide an incredible post-graduate course in the spiritual. If you desire your Millennium Doctorate in "Universe Affairs," then be grounding yourself in His Word now. Then listen for that heart-expanding greeting at the Kingdom Gate: "Well done, thou good and faithful servant . . . enter thou into the joy of the Lord" Matt. 25.

15

FALLING LIGHTNING!

"And I saw an angel come down from heaven, having the key of the bottomless pit, and a great chain in his hand. And he seized hold on the dragon, that old serpent, who is the devil, and Satan, and BOUND HIM a thousand years, and cast him into the bottomless pit, and SHUT HIM UP, and set a seal upon him, so that he should deceive the nations no more, till the thousand years should be fulfilled" Rev. 20.

What a relief!

On Jailing-Day, the planet's atmosphere will experience a sudden switch in polarity — from negative to positive! The generators of Hell switched off! Those Satanic forces we have struggled with for so long will simply disappear. No more demonic fannings of our impulses in the areas of lust, anger, fear and hate.

Holiness will be Millennium's hallmark. Those with a tendency toward sin and rebellion will be constrained. ". . . and a King shall reign and prosper, and shall execute judgment and justice in the earth" Jer. 23.

In the coming, Satan-free world, discipline will still be required among the non-glorified citizenry to avoid spiritual failure. Without further "help" from Satan they will still have to contend with that potential for evil within themselves.

Does this mean Millennium life will be darkened by their sinning? Although there will be sin among the non-glorified during the Millennium, it will be minimal. Righteousness will predominate for these reasons: (1) Satan will be chained, (2) there will be a holy environment, (3) Millennium society will be governed with a firm hand (4) Jesus will be in residence on the planet.

But, amazingly, toward the end of God's 1000-year display of near-idyllic life, trouble looms again: "And when the thousand years are expired, Satan shall be loosed out of his prison, and shall go out to deceive the nations which are in the four quarters of the earth, Gog and Magog, to gather them together to battle; the number of whom is as the sand of the sea. And they went up on the breadth of the earth, and compassed the camp of the saints about, and the beloved city" Rev. 20.

You say; "Good grief. Not again!" Yes, somehow Satan is able to recruit a big army from among the Millennium masses. They march to attack the saints in Jerusalem. Unglorified Millennium citizens who have secretly carried a sin-yearning begin to polarize around that magnet of evil. In exposing these evil-prone people, Satan concludes his final work.

The army of the wicked is destroyed: "And fire came down from God out of heaven, and devoured them. And the devil that deceived them was cast into the lake of fire and brimstone, where the beast and the false prophet are and shall be tormented day and night for ever and ever" Rev. 20.

Satan joins antichrist and false prophet, who, since Armageddon, have been waiting for him in the lake. THAT becomes THAT! Pride-choked Lucifer reaches his eternal address. God always has the final word! "And He said unto them, I beheld Satan as lightning fall from heaven" Luke 10.

PASSPORT DENIED

As we see the big picture, it becomes clear that no "sin fun" in this life is worth jeopardizing our passports to that Jesus-powered Millennium. "Choosing rather to suffer affliction with the people of God, than to enjoy the pleasures of sin for a season" Heb. 11.

May our Millennium credentials never be stamped, "PASSPORT DENIED," through failure to recognize God's attitude about holy living through Christ.

May we remember those chilling words spoken to the ungodly: "No fornicators, nor idolaters, nor adulterers, nor effeminate, nor abusers of themselves with mankind; no thieves nor covetous, nor drunkards, nor extortioners, shall inherit the Kingdom of God" I Cor. 6.

There has recently been much emphasis on LIBERTY in the Christian life, but liberty has too often skidded over into LICENSE. Too many believers are drifting into traps of situation-ethics and situation-spirituality. In this hour, so near time's edge, it's intelligent to walk the line.

> *Be ye also patient,*
> *Stablish your hearts:*
> *For the coming of the Lord draweth nigh.*
>
> — Jas. 5

16

ONE HOUR WITH GOD

Wouldn't it be breathtaking to sit down with Jesus and ask Him all about the new age? Back when the disciples asked Him about the future He responded with such patience and graciousness. It's always pleasing to the Lord when we show a sincere hunger for truth. "Blessed are they which do hunger and thirst after righteousness; for they shall be filled" Matt. 5. After Jesus had illuminated the Scriptures on the road to Emmaus, His two "pupils" sighed, "Did not our hearts burn within us, while He talked with us . . ." Luke 24.

In the very opening of Revelation we sense the Lord's honoring a press for Truth. "BLESSED is he that readeth, and they that hear the word of this prophesy, and keep those things which are written therein; for the time is at hand" Chap. 1.

There is a similar promise at the beginning of the longest Psalm, "BLESSED are they . . . that seek Him with the whole heart" Psa. 119. Believers are encouraged to ask for wisdom and, accordingly, we should never hesitate to ask the Lord for spiritual answers. He honors diligent inquiries from His own.

The Millennium will include some very illuminating decades of teaching. "Come and let us go up to the mountain of the Lord, and to the house of the God of Jacob and HE WILL TEACH US OF HIS WAYS" Micah 4.

But let's spend a hypothetical hour right now with Jesus, for a better understanding of what Millennium life will really be like:

QUESTION: "What kind of clothes will we be wearing during the Millennium?

ANSWER: "The saints will be easily distinguishable from the other strata of non-glorified Millennium people by THEIR CLOTHING, as well as by their new bodies. Only believers will be allowed to wear the 'fine linen, clean and white: for the fine linen is the righteousness of the saints' " Rev. 19. The shining white of the saints will be their distinctive privilege among all who live in the renewed earth. 'And they shall walk with me in white: for they are worthy. He that overcometh, the same shall be clothed in white raiment' Rev. 3. Again in Revelation 7, 'lo, a great multitude, which no man could number, of all nations, and kindreds, and people, and tongues, stood before the throne, and before the Lamb, clothed with white robes."

"The predominance of white may sound monotonous to you, but it won't be! Those garments of white, fashioned just for you, will be stunning! These exquisite whites will signify not only your righteousness, but also your position in My kingdom."

QUESTION: "How will we know You? What will You be wearing?"

ANSWER: "You will recognize Me, for it says of my garments, 'Thou art clothed with honor and majesty, who coverest Thyself with LIGHT as with a garment' Psa. 104."

QUESTION: "A thousand years seems so long. What will we be doing all that time?"

ANSWER: "It won't be a time of idleness. It is written, 'His servants shall serve Him' Rev. 22. Just as Adam was given responsibility over the earth, so will the redeemed be privileged to serve Me. There will be many thrilling things to fill your new life. You will rule over earth's restoration and help govern. There are many worlds to explore — you will never exhaust the intricacies of My universe. The study of My principles and ways will occupy dazzling ages to come. But don't worry, you won't feel overworked but will enjoy the bounding new energies from immortality. There will be ample opportunities for happy meetings with redeemed friends from back in time. And visits with millions from your new royal family. Then YOU AND I will have times of fellowship and we won't overlook games and leisure, either."

QUESTION: "Will we be able to see the angels?"

ANSWER: "Yes, you will see angels. Certain angels will help at the close of Armageddon. When you are changed in that 'twinkling of an eye' your vision spectrum will be wonderfully expanded. Many spirit beings are about you even now, but in your present state they aren't yet visible. I have, in special past situations, allowed saints to see angels. Glorified eyes will always be able to view them. You will even be sitting in court over certain angels: 'do ye not know that the saints will judge the world? And if the world shall be judged by you, are ye unworthy to judge the smallest matters? Know ye not that we shall judge angels?' I Cor. 6. You will delight in meeting My wonderful angelic creations who, in the past, although unseen, often ministered in your behalf. Meet the angel messenger I sent to Daniel: 'His body also was like the beryl, and his face as the appearance of lightning and his eyes as lamps of fire, and his arms and his feet like in colour to polished brass, and the voice of his words like the voice of a multitude' Dan. 10."

QUESTION: "This may seem a small thing, but I have wondered if the sounds will be any different in the Millennium."

ANSWER: "The world is now filled with many distressing, grating noises. They are the harsh sounds of a dying age. Screams, weeping, arguments, and lying will never again be heard. Many people are becoming deaf because of the loud noises characteristic of this era's final days; motorcycles, trucks, screeching tires, blaring horns, curses and screaming jets! These raucous sounds will disappear. Also the snarling, roaring and growling animals will then have new voices of contentment, reflecting their changed natures. When you hear the new Millennium instruments and harmonies they will transcend the greatest melodies ever to bathe the human soul. Even Millennium's 'quiet' will pulsate with a kind of joy and tranquility."

QUESTION: "Will everybody be the same age in the Kingdom Era?"

ANSWER: "Those who aren't glorified believers will be of various ages. 'There shall yet old men and old women dwell in the streets of Jerusalem, and every man with his staff in his hand for every age. The streets of the city shall be full of boys and girls playing' Zech 8. But among My glorified family there will be PERPETUAL youthfulness and vitality."

QUESTION: "Will Millennium citizens build houses and hold land during the new age?"

ANSWER: "Oh, yes, 'And they shall build houses and inhabit them; and they shall plant vineyards and eat the fruit of them. They shall not build, and another inhabit . . . plant, and another eat . . . and mine elect shall long enjoy the work of their hands . . . for they are the seed of the blessed of the Lord, and their offspring with them' Isa. 65.

"And so you see, there will be work and houses and fields, but it will be a pleasant, productive and enchanting life. Never again will men sweat or labor fruitlessly. The new fertility of the land, the harmony with nature and the absence of insects will make farming exciting."

QUESTION: "Many have wondered, will there be sexual relations, as we know them, during the Millennium?"

ANSWER: "There will be children born among the non-glorified mass of people. But for My own royal family there will be even greater ecstasies. The sexual aspect of human relationships has been the most perverted of all My designs for humanity. Sex has been so abused it has become a stench to My nostrils! It is not yet time for you to know the full design of the new age. But of this be assured; there will be FULLNESS OF JOY! Every good thing experienced during this present, flawed age will have a finer counterpart when you are with me. Read again the Song of Solomon, with a pure and holy heart. My patterns and principles will not be abandoned in eternity, for they are right and pleasing to Me.

QUESTION: "Since the last enemy, DEATH, isn't conquered until after Millennium, does this mean that millions will die off during this coming age?"

ANSWER: "There will be deaths among the unsaved citizens, yet death will not be found among the glorified saints: 'In a moment, in the twinkling of an eye, at the last trump . . . the dead shall be raised incorruptible, and we shall be changed. For this corruptible must put on incorruption, and this mortal must put on immortality. So when this corruptible shall have put on incorruption, and this mortal shall have put on immortality, then shall be brought to pass the saying that is written, Death is swallowed up in victory. O death, where is thy sting? O grave, where is thy victory' I Cor. 15."

QUESTION: In reading the scriptures it appears there will be differences in the rewards and the rulership assignments. These seem related to each Christian's overall spiritual performance in this present life. Wouldn't this mean that when these heavenly prizes are given out that the apostles, the Bible heroes and famous ministers will get the lion's share? What will be left for ordinary Christians?"

ANSWER: "The day in which believers' rewards are presented will bring much excitement and surprises. Some of the so-called 'big name' Christians will receive lesser rewards than expected. 'For other foundation can no man lay than that is laid, which is Jesus Christ. Now if any man build upon this foundation gold, silver, precious stones, wood, hay, stubble; Every man's work shall be made manifest: for the day shall declare it, because it shall be revealed by fire; and the fire shall try every man's work of what sort it is. If any man's work abide which he hath built thereupon, he shall receive a reward.' I Cor. 3.

"The HEART MOTIVE is a strong factor in My determination of spiritual rewards: 'That which is highly esteemed among men is abomination in the sight of God' (Luke 16); 'many that are first shall be last, and the last shall be first' (Matt. 19).

"Also, there will be amazement when I present special rewards to presently unknown men, women and children. Many who are unheralded have quietly demonstrated great spiritual valor! Their spiritual heroism is frequently unrecognized in this life — 'The meek shall inherit the earth' Matt. 5.

"Some 'little' people who were never able to lead anyone into salvation will still be found near the front in the reward line. Those who, for many years, labored in prayer while stricken with pain and even bedridden. Others will be singled out for heavenly acclaim who have allowed the Holy Spirit to develop in them a fragrant spiritual character during an earthly life filled with adversities. Heroes will be revealed who were steadfast in the midst of prison and torture. Godly women who remained aglow with the Spirit, though for many years linked to a wicked, abusing mate. Many faithful shepherds of small flocks who never knew acclaim will be given assignments of great responsibility because they proved faithful in the small things, etc. Crowning Day will ring throughout eternity!

> *Full many a gem of purest ray serene*
> *The dark, unfathomed caves of ocean bear:*
> *Full many a flower is born to blush unseen,*
> *And waste its sweetness on the desert air.*
> — Thomas Gray

QUESTION: "This, again, may seem like a tiny thing,

but I love to fish. Will there be any fishing in the Kingdom Age?"

ANSWER: "Millennium fishing will be the very best! 'And it will come about that every living creature which swarms in every place where the river goes, will live. And there will be very many fish, for these waters go there, and the others become fresh, so everything will live where the river goes. And it will come about that fishermen will stand beside it; from Eingedi to Eneglaim there will be a place for the spreading of nets. Their fish will be according to their kinds' Ezek. 47, ASV."

QUESTION: "It seems hazardous for the glorified believers to live here on earth during Millennium years, right along with those who haven't yet been changed. Won't the behavior of some tempt the glorified to sin?"

ANSWER: "No, that won't be any problem whatsoever. The glorified believer will have put off corruption and put on INCORRUPTION. By then, the glorified have been transformed and sealed against even any impure thoughts. This new and permanent INCORRUPTION will be essential so that My redeemed may safely be sent just anywhere. They will be required to rule and reign in many kinds of situations."

"Thank you, Lord."

17

SECRET OF THE INDESTRUCTIBLES

Listen now! "And they shall come and bring in the height of Zion, and shall flow unto the goodness of Jehovah, to the grain, and to the new wine, and to the oil, and to the young of the flock and of the herd: and their soul shall be as a watered garden; and they shall not sorrow anymore at all. Then shall the virgin rejoice in the dance, and the young men and the old together; for I will turn their mourning into joy" Jer. 31. Is this just melodic poetry or is it an actual and electrifying preview of a soon-coming event?

It is for real, alright. It is God's covenant promise of blessing to the Jews — one of those exquisite prophetic Scriptures with a dual time-prong. Jeremiah was not only foreseeing the Jews' entrance into the Promised Land but he also caught God's longer-range view of upcoming Millennium delights. It's as certain to happen as tomorrow morning's sunrise!

Even though the Jews have often grieved God, His love for them is unquenchable. "The Lord shall comfort Zion; He will comfort all her waste places; and He will make her wilderness like Eden, and her desert like the garden of the Lord; joy and gladness shall be found in it, thanksgiving and the voice of melody" Isa. 51. The Bible is interlaced with rich Millennial commitments for His chosen people.

Even so, there will be certain wicked Jews who must

105

first be weeded out, "For they are not all Israel, who are of Israel" Rom. 9. But what a celebration is coming for every Jew who, during the Tribulation, will resist the antichrist's seduction!

On the day of Christ's return, every Jew will instantly recognize Him as Messiah. "They shall all know Me, from the least of them to the greatest of them saith the Lord; for I will forgive them their iniquity, and I will remember their sin no more" Jer. 31.

For so long, the Jews have taken bitter persecution for being known as the people of God. But, soon now, full compensation will come to them for all that persecution!

Since the Six-Day War, when Jerusalem was fully liberated, we have seen a growing phenomenon: Early signs of the "budding of the fig tree" which Jesus said would indicate their "summer is nigh." The Lord has begun to fulfill His promise to lift the spiritual slumber of the Jews. It's happening today and it will steadily increase.

Right in the midst of the antichrist's Tribulation reign, a great Jewish revival will break out. The Bible tells about the remarkable 144,000 who sing a new song before the throne of God. (see Rev. 14)

Through the antichrist's persecutions the Jews will be readied to receive *Yeshua Ha Meshiakh* (Jesus), at last. Through the prophet Hosea, God foretold, "I will go and return to My place, till they acknowledge their offence and seek My face: in their affliction they will seek Me earnestly." By the time Jesus comes back with the saints to defeat and chain Satan, the Jews will be spiritually ripe. A most incredible event will take place. The world will see an entire nation saved in one single day! "And so ALL ISRAEL shall be saved: as it is written, There shall come out of Zion the Deliverer, and shall turn away ungodliness from Jacob" Rom. 11.

Wow! Are you ready for that?

"And I will rejoice in Jerusalem, and joy in my people:

and the voice of weeping shall be no more heard in her, nor the voice of crying" Isa. 65.

Yes, the Jews will come, in spite of their centuries-long rejection of God's Son. "Shall the earth be made to bring forth in one day? Or shall a nation be born at once? For as soon as Zion travailed, she brought forth her children ... Rejoice with Jerusalem, and be glad with her all ye that love her ... As one whom his mother comforteth, so will I comfort you; and you shall be comforted in Jerusalem. And when you see this, your heart shall rejoice, and your bones shall flourish like an herb: and the hand of the Lord shall be known toward His servants" Isa. 65, 66.

Some scholars believe David himself will return in a governing role. "And David my servant shall be king over them" Ezek. 37. Though most Bible students feel this Scripture is referring to Jesus, the seed of David, there is another facet. Surely God's beloved David himself, will be among the Millennium saints who will be ruling and reigning.

Yes, harvest day is fast-approaching, for the Jewish indestructibles. "Israel shall be saved in the Lord with an everlasting salvation" Isa. 45.

Jeremiah put it this way, "And they shall teach no more every man his neighbor, and every man his brother, saying, Know the Lord; For they shall ALL know Me, from the least of them unto the greatest of them" Chap. 31.

And so, every saint who has been filtered, tried and spiritually perfected, faces a golden future. The redeemed, both the Jew and the Gentile, will forever live with the Lord. "And the ransomed of the Lord shall return, and come to Zion with songs and everlasting joy upon their heads: They shall obtain joy and gladness, and sorrow and sighing shall flee away" Isa. 35.

Seiss' whole being was exercised when he thought about this coming new age: "The earth is now full of ailment and disorders, and in deep captivity to corruption. Yet it still has much attractiveness. Carpeted with green, girded with glorious mountains, ribboned with rivers. But this is only the OLD earth in its soiled and work-day garb, where the miseries of a deep, dark and universal apostasy from God holds sway. Think then what its regeneration must bring!

"An earth which no longer smarts and smokes under the curse of sin — an earth which needs no more to be torn with hooks and irons to make it yield its fruit — an earth where thorns and thistles no longer infest the ground, nor serpents hiss among the flowers, nor savage beasts lay in ambush to devour — an earth whose sod is never cut with graves, whose soil is never moistened with tears or saturated with human blood.

"Whose atmosphere never gives wing to the seeds of plague and death, whose ways are never blocked with armed men on their way to war — an earth that ever glows with salvation, and whose valleys know only the sweetness of God's pleasure — PARADISE RESTORED!"

John Walvoord's soul was also shaken as he rejoiced at Israel's role in the looming Kingdom Age: "God has promised Israel a glorious future and this will be fulfilled after the second advent. Israel will be a glorious nation, protected from her enemies, exalted above the Gentiles, the central vehicle of the manifestation of God's grace in the Millennial Kingdom. In the present age, Israel has been set aside, her promises held in abeyance. . . ."

Yes, the Jews will forever enjoy an intimate compartment in the heart of God. God's special love for them will become very evident to all Millennial citizenry. "And the foreigners shall stand and feed your flocks and the sons of the aliens shall be your plowmen and your vinedressers. But ye shall be named the Priests of the Lord; men shall call you the Ministers of our God; ye shall eat the riches of the nations . . . all who shall see them shall acknowledge them, that they are the seed whom the Lord hath blessed . . . He hath covered me with the robe of righteousness as a bridegroom decketh himself with ornaments" Isa. 61.

Our Lord will repay WITH HIGH INTEREST every righteous Jew who has suffered during the centuries of persecution for being known as His people. In the new age, a redeemed Jew will be a prized friend — the Bible speaks of this repeatedly: "In those days it shall come to pass that ten men shall take hold out of all languages of the nations, even shall take hold of the skirt of him that is a JEW, saying, We will go with you: For we have heard that God is with you" Zech. 8.

Paul wrote, "Now if the fall of them be the riches of the world, and the diminishing of them the riches of the Gentiles; HOW MUCH MORE THEIR FULLNESS?" Rom. 11.

When, long ago, God said He would "bless those who bless the Jews," He was expressing an eternal attitude. So it would be well to discipline our attitudes concerning God's chosen. It may stand us well as further preparation for the dawning age.

From the vantage point of eternity, believers will learn just how much we owe the eternal Jew. We should, accordingly, never be jealous of their place in God's heart but rejoice along with Him over them. "The Lord thy God hath chosen thee to be a special people unto Himself, above all people that are upon the face of the earth" Deut. 7.

Imagine how Jewish hearts will burn when the full impact of God's special love becomes fully evident to them! God is even going to sing love songs to them! "The Lord thy God in the midst of thee is mighty: He will save, he will rejoice over thee with joy; He will rest in His love, He will joy over thee WITH SINGING" Zeph. 3.

Thank you, God, for the Jews who brought down to us Your Word — Your ways — Your Son!

> *He shall cause them that come of Jacob to take root: Israel shall blossom and bud, and fill the face of the world with fruit.* — Isa. 27:6

18

SIX CRISES OF GOD

How should God have dealt with the chronic people problem? Centuries-long forebearance with humanity reveals His matchless character. By now it is clear He will complete His ages-old plan for earth, in spite of man! If instead, short-sighted man had been responsible for harmony in the universe and had all power he would have long ago pressed the earth "destruct" button.

The English word HOLY has an interesting root origin. It's derived from the Anglo-Saxon *halig, hal,* meaning "well, whole." Holiness is to Divine creation what breath is to life.

A. W. Tozer, in his book *The Knowledge of the Holy,* said, "God's first concern for His universe is its moral health, that is, its holiness. Whatever is contrary brings His displeasure. To preserve creation, God must deal with anything that would destroy it. When He arises to put down iniquity and save the world from moral collapse, He is said to be angry. Every act of judgment in the history of the world has instead been a holy move for its own preservation. The holiness of God, the judgments of God, and the health of the creation are inseparable. God's wrath is His utter intolerance of whatever degrades and destroys men. He hates iniquity as a mother hates the polio that would take the life of her child."

Earth is polluted from a 6000-year outfall of man's

unholiness. His patience in sparing earth is amazing but in that patience is buried a colossal plan. A divine pattern is at work to restore both man and his planet to the idyllic beginning.

The shadow of His ways has been evident from the start. Heaven itself opened with a perfect society. There was harmony and great purpose. The Father's galaxie "building programs" alone would have kept things exciting — a place of purposeful harmony.

Eventually a desire arose to expand this family that His joy might be still greater. But how? God's nature could never find satisfaction from mere robot-like love and obedience. Desiring a relationship of choice, God energized one of His most colossal thoughts; FREE WILL. But when He chose to incorporate this free-will design principle into creation, the potential for rebellion was also born. Each of the six great crises of God emanate from this Divine latitude.

But aren't you glad our great Lord stayed with His bold free-will concept? How much sweeter to God is our freely-given love than "automatic-reflex" love. How exciting to be creatures entrusted with our own will, rather than captive, preprogrammed "robots."

The price He has paid in creature disobedience to obtain this sweeter love has, however, been ongoing and enormous! If a lesser being had been sitting at the controls of the universe, he would long ago have washed his hands, saying, "making humans was a good try, but . . ." Not our God: He looked right through all the crises and saw eventual victory. It is because of His long-range vision that humanity has been permitted to survive, in spite of its sin. Aren't you glad He never quit on His people-creation? ". . . with Whom is no variableness, neither shadow of turning."

Satan has been the evil "quarterback" behind each one of these crises. As we briefly review these six major rebellions, marvel at His display of God-size love and persistence:

CRISIS I

, Its battle cry: "I WILL BE LIKE THE MOST HIGH."
Location: HEAVEN
Participants: ANGELS

Top-ranking Lucifer personally led the very first revolt. One-third of the heavenly family followed this Lawless One in defection from the Holy One. "Thine heart was lifted up because of thy beauty, thou has corrupted thy wisdom by reason of thy brightness: I will cast thee to the ground, I will lay thee before kings, that they may behold thee" Ezek. 28. Yes, lawlessness, in spite of a "perfect social environment." This huge band of angel outlaws was cast from God's presence. Earth itself became their "turf."

The heavenly Father brushed His hands and moved right on with His master plan . . . .

CRISIS II

Its battle cry: "YE SHALL BE AS GODS!"
Location: EDEN
Participants: ADAM AND EVE

Again, idyllic conditions. Freedom from sickness, poverty, sweat and strain. God vested earth authority in Adam and they had walks in the cool of the day. Simple rules of life were laid down by the Lord. But, Satan connived to snare Adam into violating them. A trap was set and Adam fell! After this Satanic victory, sin infected Adam and Eden. Violation cost Adam his title deed to earth. Satan had snatched it and God's curse fell upon the planet. Now humanity faced massive new obstacles. The Father had to break person-to-person contact with sin-contaminated man.

Even so, God chose to move on with His blueprint. . . .

CRISIS III

Its battle cry: "MY SPIRIT SHALL NOT ALWAYS STRIVE WITH MAN."
Location: BEYOND EDEN
Participants: ANTEDILUVIAN CIVILIZATION

God allowed many benefits to continue from the Eden Era. However, it wasn't long until that sin-virus had spread throughout the earth. "Every imagination of the thoughts of man's heart was only evil continually." The world became filled with despicable lewdness and violence. God saw such utter moral collapse that a complete new start for humanity was the only hope. Through Noah's preaching, God urged repentance and warned of coming doom. An ark of rescue was built to preserve a seed of humanity. All but Noah's family laughed at God and "revved up" their debauchery. "The earth also was corrupt before God, and the earth was filled with violence" Gen. 6. God mercifully sent the waters! And so the rebellious, diseased and violent were lost in the very deluge Noah had prophesied. Humanity came within a tiny handful of utter extinction because of its defiance.

And still, God wasn't dissuaded from the great plan. . . .

CRISIS IV

Its battle cry: "WE WILL NOT HAVE THIS MAN TO RULE OVER US!"
Location: MIDDLE EAST
Participants: ALL HUMANITY

It is incredible that God continued. His ways surely are above our ways — God is no quitter! Thousands of years went by after the flood. God's heart was touched as He watched humanity struggling in failure. People were living on a spiritual battlefield, caught in a crossfire between Satan and God Himself. He saw some whose hearts inclined toward righteousness — but they were in bondage to the Prince of this World.

"Operation Rescue" was launched! Reaching into the great treasure cabinet, He brought forth His most valuable possession, His own Son, to serve as ransom. The only "coin" sufficient for repurchase. The Son personally went to the cross to discharge our own debt for sin. This God-size plan shattered Satan's death-grip on humanity! Jesus came to destroy the works of the devil and was imminently successful.

You would think this collossal sacrifice would forever break the string of crises between God and man, but it still didn't end there. "He came first to His own and His own received Him not." They shouted, "We will not have this Man to rule over us." They crucified Him, but He rose in triumph, making a display of Satan's defeat.

The fourth terrible crisis had come and the Good Seed had been sown. The Lord pressed on. . . .

CRISIS V

Its battle cry: "THEY BLASPHEMED GOD AND REPENTED NOT OF THEIR DEEDS!"
Location: WORLDWIDE
Participants: SATAN AND THE SINNERS

Even though God's Calvary-stroke didn't bring instant Heaven, Jesus' work on planet earth bore much lasting fruit. The seeds of victory had been sown — God's victory book, the Bible, was scattered through humanity. On Pentecost the Holy Spirit filled the earth. With all of this going for humanity, trouble looms again as Satan spreads his evil until there is a global Sodom and Gomorrah!

God's justice must stand against wickedness. The vague hope that God is too kind ever to punish the unrighteous has become a deadly tranquilizer. It soothes the sinner's fears and lets him practice all pleasant iniquities while death draws nearer every day. God cannot and will not tolerate wickedness, for it would destroy His creation if allowed to spread unchecked.

And this rebellion does not end until "The great and terrible day of the Lord." History's most horrendous war — Armageddon, is stilled only by the appearance of Jesus, Himself. The sinister leader of malevolent forces is literally chained and God's fifth great rescue will then end.

The near idyllic Millennium Era opens. Jesus "sets up shop" on earth. Mankind is given a thousand Satan-free years to make up its mind about eternal allegience. The final exams then take place. . . .

CRISIS VI

Its battle cry: "WE WILL FOLLOW SATAN AND NOT THE KING!"
Location: JERUSALEM
Participants: SATAN AND THE LAST DREGS OF SINFUL HUMANITY

Note that there are Six major crises. Six is the number of incompleteness and it is also the number of HUMANITY. Man will always be frustrated and incomplete until he adds one more element to his life — JESUS. SEVEN is the number of perfection and also the number of Divinity.

When man has tried to go it alone, he has failed. Whenever he has tried to be master of his own fate and captain of his own soul, he has crashed!

Man becomes warlike, sickened and miserable when God is crowded out. The sixth and final rebellion will take place around Jerusalem. At the very end of the Millennium, Satan is again loosed to roam amongst humanity. As incredible as it seems, Satan will actually be able to recruit an army for a final war against the saints at Jerusalem. These rebellious

Millenniumites will be recruited from among the children born to the non-glorified populace. Satan and his wicked army will storm Jerusalem, itself.

Finally, God has had enough and reaches for that destruct button! Fire rains from heaven and every last rebel is forever eliminated. Satan is thrown into the lake of fire and the testing times are forever and ever behind us. Those remaining have passed their final exams and graduated into eternity.

The great circle of God is completed. His royal household has now grown to include every person, through all the ages, whose hearts inclined toward Him. A great family, tested and proven under fire. Through faith each has personally chosen to join the family of God. Full royal privileges forever extended to them by a joyous Father. . . .

"Thou art worthy, O Lord, to receive glory and honour and power: for Thou hast created all things, and for Thy pleasure they are and were created" Rev. 4.

19

PLANT OF RENOWN

"And I will raise up for them a PLANT OF RENOWN, and they shall be no more consumed with hunger in the land..." Ezek. 34. Is it startling to realize there will be farming during the Millennium? Here again, we've had such a hazy understanding of Millennium life that, I suppose, food production hasn't been considered. Some of our traditional concepts of Millennium have taken on an ethereal aura. The practicality of such basics as eating, housing and transportation have been rarely thought about.

But through Millennial Scriptures, these realities are slowly coming into focus. "Now we see through a glass, darkly; but then face to face: now I know in part, but then shall I know even as also I am known" I Cor. 13. God wants us to peer through that murky glass and take strength from the glories we see.

There will be hammering, sawing and the whir of the planter. "And they shall build houses, and inhabit them; and they shall plant vineyards, and eat the fruit of them. They shall not build, and another inhabit... They shall not labor in vain..." Isa. 65. Then through Ezekiel's Millennium pen, "... and shall build houses, and plant vineyards; yea they shall dwell with confidence..." Chap 28. Can you see the emerald green fields dotted with fabulous Millennium buildings? The fields exploding with lush Millennium flowers, fruit and grain? Birds, frolicking animals, butterflies and contented people?

TAMING OF THE SHREW

On the day God lifts earth's curse, He's going to have an important "talk" with the animal kingdom: "And I will make with them A COVENANT OF PEACE, and will cause the evil beasts to cease out of the land; and they shall dwell safely in the wilderness, and sleep in the woods" Ezek. 34. And again God speaks of this through the prophet Hosea: "And in that day will I MAKE A COVENANT for them with the beasts of the field, and with the fowls of the heavens, and with the creeping things of the ground: and I will break the bow and the sword and the battle out of the earth, and will make them to lie down safely" Chap. 2.

He will personally "covenant" with the wild things, changing their present treacherous natures. In a way, they will be "born again" to harmonize with the rest of Millennium creation.

As a direct result of God's wild animal modifications, they will never again be carnivorous. One of the wild-creature problems, since earth's curse, has been that some animals became flesh eaters. Lions, wolves and others will attack for food. When they become "vegetarians" instead of people-eaters, we'll enjoy their company more, won't we?

Joel wrote about the wonderful blessings coming to the "reformed" animals. "Fear not, oh land; be glad and rejoice: for the Lord will do great things. Be not afraid, YE BEASTS OF THE FIELD: for the pastures of the wilderness do spring . . ." Chap. 2.

Isaiah speaks of the coming harmony between the animals themselves: "The wolf also shall dwell with the lamb, and the leopard shall lie down with the kid . . . and the cow and the bear shall feed . . . and the lion shall eat straw like the ox . . . they shall not hurt nor destroy . . ." Chap. 11.

It's going to be fun getting acquainted with all the birds and animals. Man has a deep-down longing to be their friend. That's why a trip to the zoo is so much fun. For centuries man has written stories of fraternizing with the animals.

There's a special thrill when we coax a bird or a squirrel to make friends. Perhaps just a little sparrow enticed by crumbs on our window sill. Might this deep urge have come down from the Garden of Eden? Adam lived among the animals and experienced joy in that communion. He KNEW them so intimately the Lord entrusted him to name each of them. That act has a profound connotation. Restoration of man-animal relations is going to provide a very bright corner in Millennial life.

A PROPHET NAMED WALTER

You know, I think we may have had an unrecognized "prophet" at work. He was a very unusual kind of prophet from a modern-day Gomorrah called "Hollywood."

Remember wonderful Walt Disney's cartoons with the little wood's animals sitting around a campfire, swaying and clapping their hands, wagging their tails and singing? Perhaps those cartoons were prophetic. I think we may actually see that during the Millennium. The animals will even join in with us as we sing and praise the Lord. Can you hear it? "Let everything that has breath praise the Lord . . ." Psa. 150. People, animals, trees, hills and maybe even flowers getting in on the act. Wow — what a choir!

I wonder what we'll do when a friendly Millennium hippopotamus tries to sit on our lap?

Neither has God forgotten the cattle: "I will feed them in good pastures, and upon the high mountain . . . there shall they lie in a good field, in a fat pasture shall they feed . . ." Ezek. 34.

Last summer Pat Boone had a delightful foretaste of this coming harmony. Pat's eyes were wide when he told us what happened. "I was staying with my parents for a few days while doing some recording in Nashville. Early one evening I was singing, out on Mama's porch swing, all by myself. Five or ten minutes after I started to sing out there, the presence of the Lord came down in a very unique way. The songs of praise rose higher in my throat as I was caught up in worship.

"Suddenly I became aware of some new voices chiming in — a great cricket chorus was joining in with me. It was so startling that I quit right in mid-song and — you guessed it — the crickets stopped too. Hesitantly I started to sing again and once more that cricket choir joined right in on my praises."

LORD OF THE FLIES

It's still hard to visualize a perfect environment which would include mosquitoes, hornets, bees, spiders and flies, isn't it? The promise of Eden-like life certifies elimination of troublesome insects. The Bible tells how the stinger of the asp will be pulled and we know old Beelzebub, the Lord of the Flies, gets caged for a thousand years. Millenniumites can enjoy their evening lakeside picnics after all. Think you can adjust to a world without pests?

THE GOOD EARTH

There's something deeply stirring when we see magnificent stands of grain and trees laden with fruit. Have you ever seen the acres of blossoming tulips in Holland? The explosion of luxuriant trees and foliage in the South Pacific islands is breathtaking! ... Wild coconuts, bananas and papaya seem like a foretaste of Millennium. Sometimes I think those unspoiled islands are parked out there to give us a hint of verdant eternity.

Yet agronomists are worried over planet Earth's rapidly approaching incapability to feed her passenger load. Increasingly we hear of famines caused by drought, pestilence and over-population. So it's understandable if some wonder how this world could ever feed a coming, huge Millennial populace which will include saints from all generations, plus those millions of unglorified citizens.

There are going to be plenty of people alright, but there will never again be any need for concern about shortages. That pale horse of the apocolypse will be forever tied. The Scripture promises about Millennium food are magnificent! The restructured earth will by then have millions of new fertile, tillable acres. And farmers will especially appreciate the profound consequences of no more weeds, blight or devouring insects. Under this present time of the earth's curse, these combine to destroy millions of tons of food.

Perfecting of earth's climate will likewise multiply the quantity and enhance the quality of its food. "Then shall He give the rain to thy seed, that thou shalt sow the ground withal; and the bread of the increase of the earth, and it shall be fat and plenteous" Isa. 34. No more drought, floods, hail, frosts or damaging winds.

Let's review just a few of the extraordinary passages about this Millennium horn-of-plenty:

* "And I will multiply the fruit of the trees, and the increase of the field . . ." Ezek. 36.
* "But they shall sit every man under his vine and under his fig tree . . ." Micah 4.
* "So the Lord shall make bright clouds, and give them showers of rain, to every one grass in the field" Zech. 10.
* "And the desolate land shall be tilled" Ezek. 36.
* "In that day shall the branch of the Lord be beautiful and glorious, and the fruit of the earth shall be excellent and splendid . . ." Isa. 4.
* "For the seed shall be prosperous; the vine shall give her fruit, and the ground shall give her increase, and the heavens shall give their dew . . ." Zech 8.
* "And the parched ground shall become a pool, and the thirsty land springs of water . . ." Isa. 35.

FAIR AND WARMER

Not only will there be unheard of fertility but also no further time-lapses between crops. "Behold, the days come, saith the Lord, that THE PLOWMAN SHALL OVERTAKE THE REAPER, and the treader of the grapes him that soweth seed; and the mountains shall drop sweet wine . . ." Amos 9.

Even today, by utilizing the new technique of hydroponics, it is possible, in a small 40-x-180-foot plot, to grow more food than on 10 acres of ground. Using such idealized agricultural methods some remarkable products have already been grown. Eight-foot tomato plants — fruits that weigh a pound and a half — 100-pound watermelons! And Millennium farmers will make these beauties look pretty ordinary.

What is that mysterious and exciting promise God made through Ezekiel? "And I will raise up for them a PLANT OF RENOWN, and they shall be no more consumed with hunger . . ." Ezek. 34.

What will this new "plant of renown" be like? What wonder-plant is God fashioning for Millennium? Might it have the combined flavor of strawberry, banana, mango and orange? I don't know for ". . . neither hath it entered in to the heart of man the things God has prepared for them that love Him." But it will be exquisite, tasty and remarkable — a plant of renown. Exciting things lie in store for us!

20

BRIGHT GOLDEN HAZE

One of the prominent facets of Millennium life will also be one of its more illusive to understand: THE GLORY OF GOD FILLING THE EARTH!

I just wonder if, during our present state, we can ever really grasp this colossal Millennial truth? "And the GLORY OF THE LORD shall be revealed, and all flesh shall see it together" Isa. 40. ". . . Blessed be His glorious name for ever: and let the WHOLE EARTH BE FILLED WITH HIS GLORY" Psa. 72.

The Bible records instances, down through time, when the Glory and presence of Divinity was briefly exposed. "Then I beheld, and lo a likeness as the appearance of his loins even downward, fire; and from his loins even upward, as the appearance of brightness, as the colour of amber" Ezek. 8. These visitations often resulted in shattering emotional results for the humans witnessing them. When even a MESSENGER of God appeared, people fell on their faces in fear!

It will blind enemy soldiers and horses during earth's battle of climax. "In that day, saith the Lord, I will smite every horse (of the armies that contend against Jerusalem) with astonishment, and his rider with madness; and I will open mine eyes upon the house of Judah, and will smite every horse of the people with blindness" Zech. 12. Man, in his present state, can't tolerate proximity to this "electricity" from God's glory.

Moses once saw His glory as a "burning bush." At other times it appeared as a "cloud by day and a pillar of fire by night." When the Ark of the Covenant was foolishly opened, thousands perished through exposure to THE PRESENCE, (see I Sam. 6.)

Also, when Moses came down from that mountain meeting with God, his being was charged with radiated Glory. Just from Moses' nearness to it, his face had to be veiled because of an "unbearable" incandescence.

The Jews were immobilized by the Glory when it filled the traveling tabernacle: "And it came to pass, when the priests were come out of the holy place, that the Cloud filled the house of the Lord, so that the priests could not stand to minister because of the Cloud: for the GLORY OF THE LORD had filled the house . . ." I Kings 8.

Peter wanted to build three monuments when Christ appeared in His glorified state, along with Moses and Elijah, on the Mount of Transfiguration.

The glory seems to "blow fuses" in our present emotional network. Quite often Bible personalities "fainted" through awe or fear. On the Road to Damascus Paul was left blinded and trembling from the "light from Heaven" and the voice of Jesus.

After we are "remanufactured" at translation, our bodies will then be capable of rejoicing in the literal presence of His glory. It can destroy the wicked, but causes the righteous to rejoice. "Lift up your heads, O ye gates; even lift them up, ye everlasting doors; and the King of Glory shall come in. Who is this King of Glory? The Lord of hosts, He is the King of Glory" Psa. 24.

God displays certain of His glories for our benefit. "The heavens declare the Glory of God; and the firmament showeth His handiwork" Psa. 19. Throughout nature we find "glory hints" like a road sign pointing toward the full Millennial "voltage."

Let's look at a few of these "glory signs" that we can now experience in rare moments, and then imagine these amplified during every Millennial hour — never again to be just fleeting thrills. No longer to be the unusual, the exception, but the Millennial norm.

Tiny hints of that high plateau of joy that's coming: The sunshine — the tiny flower — the rainbow — an incredible sunset — springtime — northern lights — a bird song — the ever-changing sea — stars — fresh snow — the peacock — beautiful music — the rolling thunder — warm summer rain . . .

The Bible says, "He shall come down like rain upon the mown grass; as showers that water the earth" Psa. 72. When His glory comes to stay it will bring an ecstasy so intense that we must be remade at translation, even to survive.

Think of it, THE GLORY OF GOD FILLING THE EARTH!! Are you ready for that? This "bright golden haze" of the Lord's presence will bring an indescribable sense of well-being. No wonder Millennium life will be punctuated with laughter, praise and dancing! When Jesus came for that 33 incredible years He did mighty works and His glory was present at whatever place He was. In Millennium His glory won't be confined to the limited geography where He stands. Then His glory will permeate the entire planet!

THE SINGING HILLS

"For God is king of all the earth: sing ye praises with understanding" Psa. 47.

We've all felt a mysterious rousing of expectancy when *The King is Coming!* is sung. If just our anticipation can excite such a great emotional charge, imagine the wallop when we will sing, "THE KING IS HERE!"

Have you secretly wondered if it might get a little boring having so much praise time after we are with the Lord? There is nothing more dominating in Millennium prophecy than its record of the explosive, reverberating enthusiasm! Believe you me, the Millennium is going to be delightfully noisy. Our reserved emotions will melt and all will break into full-throated adoration. We "poor singers" will delight in our new Millennial voice. There will be laughter, twirling people and clapping hands and hosannas!

Some of we staid Christians will have to abandon our wooden concept of worship. We have rationalized our spiritual inhibitions by saying we want to "do things decently and in order." But the Bible tells us, "Then shall the virgin rejoice in the dance, both young men and old together; for I will turn their mourning into joy" Jer. 31. That doesn't sound too solemn and pompous. Enthusiastic worship neither embarrasses nor makes Him nervous, as it does some people.

In fact, everything cuts loose! "Let the heavens rejoice, and let the earth be glad; let the sea roar . . . let the field be joyful; then shall all the trees of the wood rejoice before the Lord" Psa. 96. Good night! The stars, the ground, the sea, the fields and the trees cutting loose in praise!

What happens when rock stars like Mick Jagger, Alice Cooper, The Rollings Stones or Elvis Presley come to town? Pandemonium, shrieks, torn clothing and even destruction — that's what. Emotional madness descends and it's like a demonic counterfeit of the coming praise and worship of the Lord. Some shrug their shoulders at the sick frenzies at rock fests. Yet these same people are horrified if someone says, "Amen" out loud in Sunday service.

People let their emotions take off when the home team scores. We jump to our feet, flail our arms and scream. (Don't worry about the spilled Coke down that fellow's neck — WE WON!) A bit of madness? Not necessarily; it's human emotions being released for a few seconds; - but for a lesser occasion than "THE KING HAS COME!" — wouldn't you agree?

Have you watched children run and leap when Daddy comes home after a trip? — kids hopping and shouting before the Christmas tree? — the enthusiastic embrace when lovers meet? Sure you have. But they're just transitory thrills, like fragile bubbles, during this present lifetime. Soon these surges of delight won't be fleeting exceptions, but permanent. If you have wondered about the high level of Millennial emotions, this is the answer. It lies in the presence of our Bridegroom.

At every glance from Jesus, our passions will break. And no wonder: "For thy love is better than wine ... The flowers appear on the earth; the time of the singing of the birds has come ... My beloved is mine, and I am his ... Thy lips are like threads of scarlet, and thy speech is comely.... Until the day break, and the shadows flee away, I will go up to the mountain of myrrh, and to the hill of frankincense. Thou art all fair, my love ... Thou hast ravished my heart ... How fair is thy love ... how much better is thy love than wine ... Thy lips ... drop like the honeycomb; honey and milk are under thy tongue; and the scent of thy garments is like the fragrance of Lebanon. A garden enclosed ... a spring shut up, a fountain sealed ... My beloved is white and ruddy, the chiefest among ten thousand. His head is like the most fine gold, his locks are bushy, and black as a raven. His eyes are like the eyes of doves ... His cheeks are like a bed of spices, like sweet flowers: his lips like lillies, dropping sweet smelling myrrh ... His legs are like pillars of marble, set upon sockets of fine gold; his countenance is like Lebanon, excellent as the cedars. His mouth is most sweet; yea, He is altogether lovely. This is my Beloved ..." Song of Solomon.

Intimate is this revelation of our own Millennium relationship with our Bridegroom. If this promise doesn't set your heart to racing, then I dare you to read it again! No wonder everything comes "unglued" with joy in the Millennium! "For ye shall go out with joy, and be led forth with peace; the mountains and the hills shall break forth before you into singing, and all the trees of the field shall clap their hands" Isa. 55.

How could the hills but sing and trees but clap? How

could our feet but dance and the little animals but leap at the very sight of Him!

"The wilderness and the solitary place shall be glad for them; and the desert shall rejoice, and blossom as the rose. It shall blossom abundantly, and rejoice even with joy and singing" Isa. 35.

But how long can such mighty ecstasy last? It will be unending: ". . . therefore shall the people praise Thee FOR EVER AND EVER" Psa. 45. "But be ye glad and rejoice FOR EVER in that which I create: . . . and the voice of weeping shall be no more heard in her, nor the voice of crying" Isa. 65.

Oh no, the love affair between Jesus and we, His bride, won't be some transitory romance. It will blossom and soar as our understanding and our capacities are enlarged. It will take us centuries to fathom His delights. The fragrance and intensity of our love will spiral higher through all the ages to come . . . .

21

SYMPHONIES IN STARDUST

*No doubt the cherubs earn their wage who wind
each ticking star.*   — Don Marquis

Out on distant planes of the universe, hidden by reefs of
time and space, lie strange realms unlike anything in our
wildest dreams. They crouch out there beyond reach of
earth-man, bizarre and unexplored . . . .

But in recent years gates into this cosmic realm have
ever so slightly begun to crack open. Recent astrophysical
breakthroughs are enabling man to catch his first tiny
glimpses of once-hidden galactic domains. These peeks have
left heretofore unflappable scientists shaken; scrambling his
notions about God, energies and origins. Time-Life recently
published a magnificent series of articles from their research
on the deterioration in our present civilization. An excerpt
from that series entitled *Second Thoughts About Man* says:
"Man's confidence in his power to control his world is
suddenly at a low ebb. The scientists themselves are now
depressed to realize that their universe is far more complex
than they recently thought and that they have fewer
solutions than hoped."

What has shattered these scientists serenity and smug-
ness? Here's what: They've discovered that far out there in
the wild, wonderful cosmos there are such things as:

* Mysterious "black holes" . . .
* Baffling tiny orbs, ashine with the power of a trillion suns . . .
* Stardust, cosmic rays and collapsed stars wandering silently . . .
* Million-mile-an-hour solar winds . . .
* Stars singing, each with their own voices (Job 38) . . .
* Super novaes like celestial fireworks . . .

Yes, the heavens declare the glory of God" Psa. 19. For eons His finger has been inscribing a cosmic testimony. The writing in the heavenlies tell of mysteries with deep spiritual and practical relevance to every believer. Let's examine a few of God's celestial wonders:

QUASARS — Small, jewel-like bodies packed with more energy than ten entire galaxies the size of our own. In one minute some quasars emit enough power to supply all of the earth's needs for 50 million years.

SUPER NOVAE — The most dramatic of cosmic fireworks! Exploding stars spreading gas clouds, meteoric fragments and scintillating dust over millions of space miles. Fiery displays so grandiose they can be ogled for 300 years.

PULSARS — Neutron stars spinning at enormous speeds which somehow emit their signals in pulses. Pulsars are so dense one thimbleful weighs more than 50,000 locomotives.

Present-generation physicists are staggered by mounting evidence of the universe's size. Astrophysical devices are now sucking in breathtaking new information about deep space. Just one, the Pioneer 10 spacecraft, has radioed back 25 billion computer bits of cosmic data. If Galileo could see the present array of instruments available to modern-day astrophysicists he would turn green with envy:

* The huge 200-inch Mt. Palomar optical telescope . . .
* Radio telescopes with acres of spidery antennae . . .
* Instrumented spacecraft like Skylab, the Mariner and Pioneer series . . .

* High-flying observatory aircraft . . .
* Batteries of computers spectrometers and exotic "black boxes" to help translate the freaky messages of starlight . . .

What magnificent tools! But what is causing some to gasp as the data rolls in? For one thing they are just beginning to fathom the scope of the universe. We are now cruising along at a cool 66,000 miles an hour, orbiting the sun on a planet which poet Archibald MacLeish described as "a small planet . . . of a minor star . . . off at the edge of an inconsiderable galaxy." On this small planet scientists labor feverishly to prove Rene Descartes' proclamation true. The haughty philosopher bragged: "There is nothing so far removed from us as to be beyond our reach; or so hidden that we cannot discover it."

But the Bible speaks of men such as Descartes, "the mouth of fools poureth out foolishness" Prov. 15. And God always has the final word.

Instead of providing an answer, this new torrent of cosmic data leaves scientists ever more baffled. Physicists listen today with new awe as their own instruments whisper of the universe's scope . . .

Gigantic heavenly galaxies, common as sands on a shore! A mind-splitting BILLION of them! No wonder confusion is king among some in the intellectual community. Little wonder there is a cringing at what the heavens are broadcasting. It's about time men listen to what those stars are trying to tell them about their Creator. But don't hold your breath, for even to the keenest NATURAL mind, these secrets will only breed still more controversy, for the Bible says, "none of the wicked shall understand . . ." Dan. 12. Until time itself ends, those trusting exclusively in their own understanding will be in confusion. They will generate more and more vain theories so long as they ignore the Bible, which is, among other things, an accurate book of science too.

Let's look a bit at their confusion: Nobel Prize winner, George Wald, has written, "I think there is no question in

that we live in an inhabited universe that has life all over it."
Wald has a lot of distinguished company who concur in this
position.

Yet others, with equal scientific credentials, insist
"There's not a shred of evidence that there is life out there in
space."

Yes, the non-spiritual community is in disarray and not
just concerning life on other planets, but also as to the origin
of the universe. For instance, hundreds of eminent physicists
hold to a steady-state universe theory, while hundreds more
cling to the "Big Bang" theory. These latter scholars presume
that, eons ago, a cataclysmic explosion occurred! They claim
that, as a result, the whole universe is rushing outward at
fantastic speed. In time, they theorize, all this matter will
implode. Everything reversing direction and racing back into
one dense mass — only to repeat the whole process, time and
again — like some bouncing ball.

What a bizarre explanation! I wonder if anyone ever
asked them, "Who put the explosives out there in the first
place and who lit the fuse?"

You can be glad if this "Big Bang" theory seems
ridiculous to you. "In the beginning God . . ." is a much
more logical conclusion. There is a special kind of wisdom
among believers which operates ABOVE the intellectual
plane. Jesus described it this way, "It is given unto you to
know the mysteries of heaven, but to them (the carnal and
unbelieving) it is not given" Matt. 13.

Yes, the Bible has a better idea: "by understanding hath
He established the heavens."

If a man does not keep pace with his companions,
perhaps it is because he hears a different drummer.
Let him step to the music he hears, however
measured or far away.
                                            — Henry David Thoreau

22

COSMIC THUNDER

Yes, the cosmos is grudgingly opening her secrets. Will we ever detect the edge of the universe? NASA is scheduled to fire into orbit a Large Space Telescope (LST) in 1983. The LST is a magnificent 120-inch telescope that will be carried into space by our new Space Shuttlecraft. Astronomers around the world are eagerly awaiting this launch since it will station Large Space Telescope in the crystalline atmosphere high above earth's smudge.

They calculate that LST will be capable of looking ten times farther into space. Astronomers hope it will enable them to view the EDGE of the universe. Before mighty LST is ever turned on, I predict disappointment.

Our God and His universe are beyond measuring with the puny instruments of men. "Where wast thou when I laid the foundations of the earth? Declare, if thou hast understanding ... Knowest thou the ordinances of heaven? Canst thou set the dominion thereof in the earth?" Job 38.

Yes, the works of God are too colossal! How can mortal man ever expect to plumb infinity. We applaud the magnificent achievements of the scholars and scientists. But some of their feverish efforts to disprove God remind me of the Shakespearean character who said, "Methinks thou protesteth too much."

God has forthrightly declared the origin of life and yet many extend to the limits of lunacy in their efforts to tread down God's explanation. "Great men are not always wise . . ." Job 32.

The contortions some scholars put themselves through to disprove God's Word border on humor. They struggle through tortured theories to discount the Bible.

"Who changed the truth of God into a lie . . ." Rom. 1.

Many who are otherwise intelligent, have psyched themselves into believing things like this bizarre theory of man's orgin: "Three and one half billion years ago a violent celestial storm broke. Thunder, lightning and solar radiation stirred a 'primoridal soup.' Out of this came amino acids, and from the brew, life-forms began to 'invent themselves'."

Can't you just see those little amino-acid molecules running around until they accidently "self-invent" an optical system, a heart, a brain, and love! Methinks they protest God too much. It doesn't require a towering intellect to recognize intellectual confusion. "Thus saith the Lord, thy redeemer, and He that formed thee from the womb, I am the Lord that maketh all things; that stretcheth forth the heavens alone; that spreadeth abroad the earth by Myself; that frustrateth the tokens of the liars, and maketh diviners mad; that turneth wise men backward, and maketh their knowledge foolish" Isa. 44.

Plato wrote, "Astronomy compels the soul to look upward." The grandeur, variety and magnitude of the celestial menagerie excites my passion for God. "For as the heavens are higher than the earth, so are my ways higher than your ways, and my thoughts than your thoughts" Isa. 55.

The sheer SIZE of creation "shorts out" human comprehension! A light beam speeding 186,000 miles every second takes 1000 years just to cross our own galaxy. And by now we know there are more than a BILLION other galaxies! So it shouldn't be surprising that God has fashioned some exotic cosmic mysteries. Each creation making Him grander and still more glorious to me.

Those recently discovered "black holes" are extremely fascinating. They exert such massive pull, everything within a million miles is sucked inside to be forever trapped. Some astronomers theorize that, at one time, they were huge bodies and they have undergone a gravitational collapse. Compressed to such density their gravity warps space and time which fold in on each other. But "black holes" are so mysterious no one really understands them.

Since their enormous pull prevents even light from escaping, they can only be detected by X-ray. Dr. Thorne of the California Institute of Technology says, "We will never be able to see inside a "black hole," and we can never know what has happened inside, since no energy, in any form, ever comes out to carry the information."

Strange indeed! Could it be some of these so-called "black holes" out in space may prove to be places for beings consigned to outer darkness? Could one of them be the bottomless pit? No one knows. Maybe when we attend Jesus University, we can find out their real purpose in God's universal economy.

The voices of the stars even now are joined in a celestial choir. Long ago the Bible said, "When the morning stars sang together . . ." Job 38. And they are singing a vital message right into our radio telescopes.

Somewhere out there is a dazzling compartment. The most deluxe territory in all the universe according to those Bible heroes who have seen it. Paul and John the Revelator, for example. Lavish with priceless stones, gold and crystal. The control center for everything that is. It's God's office and His residence. "Is not God in the height of heaven? And behold the height of the stars, how high they are!" Job 22. We will be staying there with Jesus during the Tribulation years and it would be heartbreaking to leave if we weren't returning to earth with the One who carries Heaven with Him — Jesus, the Son.

FASTEN YOUR SEATBELT

Some months ago, I was studying a group of Scriptures which reveal our relationship with the rest of creation. The Heavenly Father states flatly all things in Heaven and in earth are put under Jesus. Then we are told, "we are the children of God . . . the heirs — heirs of God, and joint-heirs with Christ . . ." Rom. 8. For still further confirmation we read in Psalm 8: "When I consider Thy heavens, the work of Thy fingers, the moon and the stars . . . What is man, that thou art mindful of him? . . . THOU MADEST HIM TO HAVE DOMINION OVER THE WORKS OF THY HANDS: THOU HAST PUT ALL THINGS UNDER HIS FEET." This exciting Scripture is repeated in the New Testament (Heb., Chap. 2).

Suddenly the implications of that message exploded! The Lord is clearly telling of our own eternal involvement with ALL OF HIS UNIVERSE. We must stretch our vision to encompass probable assignments in God's colossal space realms during eternity.

This started me thinking of some logistical problems such travels would present. I said, "Lord, It will take too long to get out there to the far reaches of Your skies. Even at the blinding speed of light it takes 1000 years to cross our own little galaxy. Since You have created at least a billion more it would consume my eternity just to travel out there on assignments. How could this problem ever be solved?"

Within seconds a question entered my mind. "What is the fastest thing you can think of in all the universe?" As I was pondering this, I thought of lightning, the speed of comets and light at 186,000 miles-a-second. I said, "Light is the fastest." Then another mental nudge. "No, light is too slow — keep thinking."

Finally it struck. Why of course, there is something faster — the speed of THOUGHT!

Suddenly I saw how it would be possible for us to fulfill eternity-assignments JUST ANYWHERE. Wow!

Imagine the might and power of our Creator to adorn the universe with a trillion massive planets, stars and celestial mysteries. Who with incomparable Divinity has hung it all on nothing. Mysteriously turning with interlocking orbit; like some colossal mobile!

"He stretcheth out the north over the empty place, and hangeth the earth upon nothing ... The pillars of heaven tremble and are astonished at his reproof ... By his spirit he hath garnished the heavens ... Lo, these are parts of his ways: but how little a portion is heard of him? But THE THUNDER OF HIS POWER who can understand?" Job 26.

23

INVASION OF THE OVERCOMERS

At the peak of the fury of the Battle of Armageddon the warriors will be suddenly awestruck at the most dramatic sight earthlings have ever seen. They will stare skyward at this sight which would pale even the most bizarre science-fiction ever written. Listen to the apostle John's description of it:

"And I saw heaven opened, and behold a white horse; and He that sat upon him was called Faithful and True ... His eyes were as a flame of fire, and on His head were many crowns ... and He was clothed with a vesture dipped in blood: and His name is called The Word of God. And the armies which were in heaven followed Him upon white horses, clothed in fine linen, white and clean ... and He hath on His vesture and on His thigh a name written, King of Kings and Lord of Lords" Rev. 19.

This spine-tingling invasion from outer space will be made up of a colossal army of spiritual "good guys" who back up their commander, Jesus Christ. Baseball great, Leo Durocher, coined a slogan, "Good guys finish last." But, as this big army invades earth it will forever disprove Leo's catchy nonsense about the good guys. Believers have been portrayed as squares and losers for too long. Jesus and these returning saints will be living proof that, in the end, Christians are big, big winners! This world will never be compatible with the Believer until it is seized by these heavenly forces and made habitable for the righteous. This place can't really be our home until Jesus "fumigates" its sin.

God issued a basic command ordering humankind to subdue and replenish the earth. Adam was ordered to "take dominion." God still expects us to be stewards of earth's physical resources, as well as spiritual treasures. This has never changed, even though Satan is still prince of this world. We have been commissioned to occupy until Christ returns. We should be spiritual occupiers and commandos. It isn't enough for us to receive God's gift of salvation and then just relax or hide out until Christ returns. After salvation, He expects us to learn His principles of spiritual warfare — then apply them. We are being trained in this life to exercise stewardship of all God provides for us: possessions, time and talents (see Luke 16.) And He expects believers to develop a "can-do" spiritual posture. The believer should be like a warrior on the attack — taking new ground. We are being watched and tested by the Lord in this life.

Jesus shared a revealing parable with His followers about a certain Nobleman who went away to receive a kingdom. In this parable, each of the servants were entrusted with one pound and told to "Occupy until I come." The pound representing the time, money, talents and the spiritual opportunities each Believer encounters during this lifetime.

When the Nobleman returned, each of the servants (representing us) were called before him. The first servant said, "Lord, Thy pound hath gained ten pounds." The master said, "Well, thou good servant: because thou hast been faithful in a very little, HAVE THOU AUTHORITY OVER TEN CITIES" Luke 19.

But one servant foolishly hid his pound. He was like the Christian who receives salvation, and then just sits on his spiritual potential. The master was anything but pleased and ordered the unused pound to be seized and given to the servant who had been so aggressive and profitable with the master's provision. It seems clear from Jesus' parable that our reigning positions during the Kingdom Age will be determined by our spiritual performance in this life.

EXCELLENT POSITIONS AVAILABLE

There will be high "management" openings for can-do Christians during Millennial civilization. Jesus is now silently recruiting those demonstrating capability as overcomers. He needs saints who develop success patterns in this present real-life testing ground, through their application of His spiritual principles. The Lord has published a valuable "how-to" manual. It's called the Bible! By practicing its spiritual formulas, we can be converted from chronic losers into consistent winners. "That ye would walk worthy of God, who hath called you unto His Kingdom and glory" I Thes. 2.

Many leaders will be needed to reign over cities, nations, territories and Millennium projects. We are NOW training for these Kingdom Age assignments. "Let a man so account of us as ... stewards of the mysteries of God. Moreover, it is required of stewards THAT A MAN BE FOUND FAITHFUL" I Cor. 4.

And don't be surprised when, during the Kingdom Age, we find some little-known Christians reigning in positions of great honor and scope. We may remember some as a "little" people who labored quietly for the Lord.

God marks those who learn to wield spiritual victory weapons. The Bible says, "The weapons of our warfare are not carnal but mighty through God to the pulling down of strongholds." Jesus paid a price that we who believe might be potent on this planet. "They overcame him by the blood of the Lamb, and by the word of their testimony." Neither heavenly prizes nor Millennial positions will be given to the fearful and unbelieving. We are designed for such power that the "gates of hell" shall not prevail against us. We are being groomed to assume leadership roles in His universe by learning spiritual disciplines.

Olympic champions must not only have talent, but discipline in order to become winners. The prizes for disciplined believers are dazzling. In Revelation is showcased a display of those glittering spiritual trophies. They will soon be awarded to Christians who purpose, during this lifetime, to let the Holy Spirit develop them into overcomers. Here is a partial array of God's prizes for the overcomer:

* "He that overcomes will I give to EAT OF THE TREE OF LIFE, which is in the midst of the paradise of God."
* He that overcomes will I give to eat of the HIDDEN MANNA."
* He that overcomes will I give POWER OVER THE NATIONS ... and I will give him THE MORNING STAR."
* "He that overcomes shall be clothed in WHITE RAIMENT."
* "He that overcomes I will CONFESS HIS NAME before my Father and before His angels."
* "He that overcomes will I MAKE A PILLAR in the temple of My God."
* "He that overcomes will I grant to SIT WITH ME IN MY THRONE, even as I also overcame."
* "He that overcomes shall INHERIT ALL THINGS."

Yes, God is now training His children for victory under the tutelage of the Holy Spirit. Developing overcoming skills requires spiritual understanding and great discipline. It also takes practice in real life situations. We are in mortal combat with unseen forces and the stakes in this battle are eternal. "We wrestle not against flesh and blood, but against principalities, against the rulers of the darkness of this world, against spiritual wickedness in high places" Eph. 6.

To fully prepare for our role in Christ's invading army, we must develop skills with our spiritual weapons and armor (Eph. 6.) As returning earthlings, our Armageddon battle cry must be, "More than conquerors through Him that loved us!"

After we have put earth aright as rulers and reigners with Jesus, perhaps He will then allow us to turn our gazes toward the galaxies.

> *Lord of all being, throned afar,*
> *Thy glory flames from sun and star;*
> *Before Thy ever-blazing throne*
> *We ask no luster of our own.*
>
> — Oliver Wendell Holmes

24

SUPERWORLD!

The Twentieth Century rages toward its close; the deadliest, stormiest and most despairing years in all history. But look . . . there's a cloud forming on the horizon, but this time it's a sliver one! Good times are headed for this planet and all the king's horses and all the devil's angels can't stop it.

". . . behold, one like the Son of Man came with the clouds of heaven . . . And there was given Him dominion, and glory, and a Kingdom, that all people, nations, and languages, should serve him: His dominion is an everlasting dominion, which shall not pass away, and His Kingdom that which shall not be destroyed" Dan. 7. The Noble One is coming soon, as vindicator of His Word and vindicator of His people.

For endless centuries men have dreamed of creating an ideal world — a Shangri-La. First, the Babylonians, then the Egyptians, the Greeks and the Romans. All followed, in more recent times, by the British, the Nazis, the Communists and even the Americans. Each with frenetic drive to usher in their own brand of global utopia. But one after another has ended in dust, smoke, slavery or Watergate!

There are some jarring ruts still ahead, as humanity road stretches toward that silver Millennium horizon. Today the world is convulsing from a terminal case of "Sin-fever." Things are getting pretty "hairy" — inflation, drugs, environmental poisoning and terrorists shopping for atomic bombs!

Something big is in the air and even a fool can sense the game is about up.

Masses are groping for either salvation or suicide. Others try to drown their despair with alcohol. Here's why: In decades past orators could weave a compelling tapestry of a glowing future for mankind. "Soaring education and sky-rocketing technology will bring a chicken in every pot, two cars in every garage, unheard of prosperity — see it just ahead?"

But that promised future finally arrived, and instead of being the glittering one promised, it was leaden: Hiroshima, Hanoi, Bangladesh and the Golan Heights. The Twentieth-Century staggers set in — the fate of our planet hangs in the balance. The orators' golden horizons have turned ominously dark.

A perplexed world stands leaderless and faint. The Bible warns against just such uncertainty. "Without a vision, the people perish."

And so, in the dusk of a dying age, that newly-forming silver cloud is a sight to behold! The good news of Millennium reality must now be heralded — its wonders polished to an accurate brilliance. Millennium, with Jesus at its helm, is the very Superworld which has eluded civilization while man has been at the wheel.

We must bring its nearness into focus — just look at it! Vibrancy, rest, peace, dancing and laughter. "Peace on earth, good will toward men."

I can see Millennium through that colossal door called TIME which is slowly, irreversibly, swinging shut. Jesus is the door and He's calling to the people on the smoking planet, "I offer life — abundant and eternal! Hurry — don't waste precious time looking for another WAY into Superworld Kingdom. I am the only WAY. Come, — the Millennium bells are ringing . . ."

Believers must sound the very good news that the WAY is still open. Compel them to safety before the WAY closes.

It's an hour to let the Holy Spirit ignite one last spiritual revolution! The fire of the early church must be kindled! Long before SLA radical, Field Marshall Cinque, put a bullet in his skull, thousands of Jesus-Radicals were praising God as the Colosseum lions snarled.

Book-of-Acts Christians weren't ashamed to be counted with their leader, Jesus Christ. Their Spirit-inspired zeal turned the world upside down! Jesus is worth making spiritual revolution for! "Behold, the Lord cometh with ten thousands of his saints."

It's time to change — we're on a sinking world. Why hide the Jesus-Lifeboat? Let's "go public" with the news of Jesus' Kingdom!

Men seem to have lost their fear of God. It's no time to "stonewall" against God. Soon the swingers and the do-your-own-thingers will discover, one heartbeat too late, that Jesus isn't the emaciated, effeminate, pitiful, dead figure on the crucifix. Their laughter will freeze as they face a blazing-eyed, omnipotent, brilliant, authoritative, live Jesus. ". . . and I will not allow them to pollute My holy name anymore" Ezek. 39.

It's time to go radical for righteousness — to declare war against sin and Satan — to "make waves" for Jesus! Never again to be timid about our allegiance to that One who hung the stars in space. We're His authorized representatives — His agents on this planet. Let our blood run hot against sin. "I will not rest, until the righteousness thereof go forth as brightness, and the salvation thereof as a lamp burneth" Joel. Yes, "Mine eyes have seen the glory of the coming of the Lord . . ."

Time to sound the final alert for all desiring Millennium passports. Planet earth is about to be "born again!" "The kingdoms of this world are become the kingdoms of our Lord; and He shall reign forever and ever" Rev. 11. Hosannas to the Father, to the Son, and to the Holy Ghost!

Those early streaks in the eastern sky herald Millennium's dawn — a romantic 1000-year-long valentine from a loving God.

> *O for a thousand tongues to sing*
> *My great Redeemer's praise,*
> *The glories of my God and King,*
> *The triumphs of his grace!*